FOUND
TREASURES

Other books by Linda M. Clark

5 Leadership Essentials for Women:
Developing Your Ability to Make Things Happen

Awaken the Leader in You: 10 Life Essentials for Women in Leadership

Dr. Linda M. Clark

FOUND
TREASURES
DISCOVERING YOUR WORTH IN UNEXPECTED PLACES

Randi,
God bless you as
you think about treasures
& how He can use them
Linda M. Clark

NEW HOPE
PUBLISHERS
Gospel-Centered. Missions-Driven.

BIRMINGHAM, ALABAMA

New Hope® Publishers
PO Box 12065
Birmingham, AL 35202-2065
NewHopeDigital.com
New Hope Publishers is a division of WMU®.

Library of Congress Control Number: 2013955346

All Scripture quotations, unless otherwise indicated, are taken from King James
Version.
     Scripture quotations marked AMP are taken from the Amplified® Bible,
Copyright © 1954, 1958, 1962, 1964, 1965, 1987 by The Lockman Foundation. Used
by permission.
     Scripture quotations marked *The Message* are taken from *The Message* by Eugene
H. Peterson. Copyright © 1993, 1994, 1995, 1996, 2000, 2001, 2002. Used by
permission of NavPress Publishing Group.
     Scripture quotations marked NIV are taken from the HOLY BIBLE, NEW
INTERNATIONAL VERSION®. NIV®. Copyright©1973, 1978, 1984, 2011 by
Biblica, Inc.® Used by permission. All rights reserved worldwide.
     Scripture quotations marked NKJV are taken from the New King James
Version. Copyright © 1982 by Thomas Nelson, Inc. Used by permission. All rights
reserved.
     Scripture quotations marked NLT are taken from the *Holy Bible,* New Living
Translation, copyright © 1996. Used by permission of Tyndale House Publishers,
Inc., Wheaton, Illinois. All rights reserved.

ISBN-10: 1-59669-411-4
ISBN-13: 978-1-59669-411-8

N144117 · 0714 · 2M1

FIND THESE:

Found Treasures QR Codes

You can scan the QR codes in this book to find color photos of the author's found treasures (black and white photos are at the end of each chapter). Whether you read *Found Treasures* on your own, with a friend, or with a small group, simply use your mobile device and a QR code reader to connect with content, and Linda Clark's found treasures.

DEDICATION

To the special women in my life whose encouragement has helped me develop a healthy self-esteem: Debra, Ethel, Cate, and Mama. And, to the One whose sacrificial life and acceptance of me affirms my worth in His eyes.

CONTENTS

INTRODUCTION

WHEN IS THE LAST TIME YOU LOOKED IN A MIRROR? To check your makeup as you left for work? To see how your new dress looked? To make sure that your lipstick matches your blouse? To admire your new haircut? To adjust the necklace you found that's become a special treasure?

Of the many judgments we make, perhaps none is more important than the one we make about ourselves! The reflection we see is very important because it can influence every aspect of our lives. It can determine our behavior, relationships, and performance. It often dictates our ability to make decisions, to love, and to take risks even in the face of failure. Nearly all of us have thought (or even made) the following statements about our abilities: "I'm about the same as everyone else. I've got some good points and some things I need to work on." "I'm perfect! Why can't everyone else be as good as I am?" "I can't do anything right. I'm just no good. Everyone else is much better than I am."

The image we try to show others is not necessarily the way we actually are. Others' perceptions of our abilities and accomplishments may be accurate or very misleading! Is self-esteem really this intrusive in our lives? Why even discuss something as personal as the way we see ourselves? A basic beginning point is understanding that our self-esteem is not a secret, something hidden in the dark recesses of our minds and hearts. Whether we realize it or not, our self-esteem is "out there," and those who interact with us either confirm or negate our perception of ourselves. While she is an extremist in many ways, Gloria Steinem hit the nail on the head with her statement about self-esteem, "Self-esteem isn't everything; it's just that there's nothing without it."

So, if this book is about building healthy self-esteem, why is the book entitled *Found Treasures*? What in the world does that have to do with self-esteem? In fact, what is a "found treasure"? Let me tell you how I reached this point.

A children's librarian by profession, my friend Frances was a woman with many interests. She had a passion for instilling in children a love for books and the adventures they could have through the printed page. Her summer reading programs were testimonies to her creativity as hundreds of youngsters were motivated to spend their summer days journeying to the past, traipsing through visiting fantasy lands, examining other people's lives, and becoming mystery detectives.

While her library activities were primary, Frances had a life outside of its walls. She participated in the women's groups in her church and was a member of the local chapter of the business/professional women's service club. Later in life, she became interested in embroidery and attended many instructional seminars that led her to launch new projects demonstrating her newly learned skills. From firsthand observation, I knew there were more projects launched than completed at times!

One time, while I was visiting her home, she began showing me all of her latest projects. One was a black lacquered box with a recessed area in its lid. When I asked what it was, she responded by giving me the details of the latest embroidery class she had attended. The class was called Found Objects and featured taking an object that the stitcher had found and turning it into an ornamental element of a box, a piece of jewelry, or framed picture. Frances's found object was a small stone she found on one of her vacations. The class instructor had taught attendees how to attach objects such as shells, stones, feathers, metal pieces, or scraps of paper to fabric and then embellish the fabric to showcase the object.

Intrigued, I began to research the found objects idea. I discovered that the art of found objects is not limited to stitchery projects. Many artists create fanciful pieces from clay or paint adding found objects to their work. Quilters incorporate found objects into wall hangings and other textile works. This new information spurred me to email my brother, a professional musician. He is a member of several musical groups and plays a variety of instruments. I remembered he had been given an unusual instrument called the "Crustacean" by its creator. When I questioned him if it would qualify as a found object, he didn't think so because it was made from already manufactured materials. Since he composes music and has his own recording studio, I inquired if my brother had ever used found objects in his music.

I think he was curious to find out what his sister was up to because his reply came back quickly! It read, "The more traditional definition of a found object in music would be like a percussionist who used a found hubcap or can and banged around on it. Another example would be, say, a turtle shell that has dried out and someone uses it for an instrument. I heard someone make some great music with different lengths of tubes or hoses he found and whirled them around his head like a lasso. They made really interesting sounds."

My brother has done a lot of compiling of sounds that he considers to be found objects in the larger sense of the term. He has used a recorded bird, water, and crowd sounds and incorporated them into compositions. "Even though they are not material found objects, I think they qualify as sound found objects," he told me.

As I have worked with women through the years, I have met many who were self-assured and confident in their abilities. I also have met women who were searching, not always successfully, for their niche in life. Their identities were often tied to their past, their expectations were low, and they could not function confidently in their relationships with their families, communities, or in their churches. Their perceptions of their abilities were tainted by others' opinions, and they had a difficult time seeing themselves as individuals of worth to God and others. Building and maintaining healthy self-esteem is in itself a lifetime journey that every woman takes. There are many twists and bends along the way—even some U-turns!

Not long ago as I was traveling, I began to think about some of my found objects. I realized that while they had little or no monetary value, the place I found them or the object itself had special meaning to me. As I reflected on the objects I had gathered through several years, I realized I could connect all of them to elements of a woman's self-esteem. Thus, I began a creative journey to tell the stories of some ordinary things and what I have learned from them. It is my hope that you, too, will find meaning in ordinary objects and be able to relate them to your personal journey toward a healthy self-esteem and joy in Christ. Enjoy and grow!

(Note: The quotes from my brother, Bill Bell, were from an email I received from him in response to my inquiry about music and found objects on August 31, 2011.)

COME AND SEE!

IT'S ALWAYS AN EXCITING THING FOR ME TO GO TO A library. It has been an adventure ever since I was a child looking for a new "read." Summers were filled with reading programs and discoveries of new authors. My favorites for several years were biographies which were bound in bright pumpkin-orange covers. I knew adventures were ahead when I found one of those orange books!

When I begin thinking about my journey to a healthy self-esteem, I am certain I have read several books along the way that gave me ideas about what self-esteem is and how one can move toward a healthier view of oneself. However, I want to assure you that I have not arrived at the ultimate healthy self-esteem. That notion could not be further from the truth! I really believe that none of us ever comes to a place where we feel secure in all of the areas that relate to self-esteem. Some days I feel really good about myself; other days, not so much. My search for information about self-esteem led me to several libraries, so I knew there were exciting times ahead! Did I mention I love libraries and books?

I discovered, as I pulled numerous books from the shelves, that a lot of people have their own definition of *self-esteem*. The authors' conclusions are all related—no question about that—but they vary just enough that I think it will be good for me to make some comments at this point before we begin our investigation into a subject that is important to all of us. *Merriam-Webster's Collegiate Dictionary*, 11th Edition, defines *self-esteem* as "a confidence and satisfaction in oneself." Bruce Narramore, founding dean of the Rosemead School of Psychology at Biola University, says, "Our attitude toward ourselves . . . is one of the most important things we possess. It is the source of our personal happiness or lack of it. It establishes the boundaries of our accomplishment and defines the limits of our fulfillment."

Well! These definitions alone would be enough to keep us talking for a long time, wouldn't they? I propose you take a few minutes to search a dictionary—print or online—and see what other definitions you can find for *self-esteem*. Look at books on self-esteem at your local library. *Wait! Cancel that idea!* You will quickly discover that while the practical parts of developing healthy self-esteem may be sound, the philosophies of authors writing from a secular perspective might be way off base. For example, one book I found had a title and contents that seemed fine. Once I got to reading, however, I realized the author was trying to convince her readers that it didn't matter who your spiritual guide was. You could increase your positive self-esteem by focusing on your inner core and thinking positive thoughts. Hmmm! Take comments such as these with the proverbial grain of salt. A better suggestion is to visit a Christian bookstore. Books you'll find there are usually biblical in approach. No matter where you get your books, unpack them with discernment! Gather several definitions you like and put them alongside the ones I've given. See if they are similar or if they are contrary to what *Webster's* and Narramore said. (I'm going to give you an example of off-base thinking in a few pages. Stay with me until then.)

You may not have done a lot of thinking about your self-esteem. Perhaps you are just moving through your days not realizing how much your opinion of yourself affects your decisions and responses to others. We all have a tendency to think we can feel good about ourselves through our own efforts. Have you discovered that you never quite measure up? You reach a goal but still don't feel worthy or loved? Is the pleasure in the accomplishment short-lived? Why is this? I believe it's because feeling good about myself is really only a "knockoff" of God's peace. When my self-esteem is connected to what I do through my own efforts, the results are unstable and not lasting. Women are deceived into thinking that it is what we do, who we are, how much money we make, how much stuff we own, or how many degrees we've earned that determine our worth.

You won't find the term *self-esteem* in the Bible, but you will find many references about our relationship to God, how He sees us, and how He loves us. The security we search for—and can find—is Jesus' shed blood. Look up these verses and read them aloud: 2 Corinthians 5:21; Ephesians 1:4; 2:9; Romans 8:15; 8:17; Galatians 3:26, 29; 1 Peter 2:9; Ephesians 2:10; Romans 8:1; and 1 Corinthians 3:9. Did you find a recurring theme? The sacrifice Jesus made for us secures us forever as God's heirs. Accepting His value of us sends us into everyday life assured of His presence and guidance.

When we accept that we have value in God's eyes, we will be able to live a complete life the way God wants us to live.

Leonard Sweet, in his book *The Jesus Prescription for a Healthy Life*, wrote, "He offers us whole life. Not half life. But full life. Life lived to its limits." Who doesn't want to live life this way? While it's important, our highest goal in life shouldn't be feeling good about ourselves. It should be to live it as Paul says in Philippians 1:21, "For to me to live is Christ."

Want to investigate this a bit more?

Turn to Psalm 139:7–16 (NIV) and read what David has to say. Then respond to the following questions:

1. What does David mean when he says, "Even the darkness will not be dark to you"?

2. David talks about being knit together in his mother's womb in verse 13. What is he talking about?

3. What does "My frame was not hidden from you" mean? (v. 15)

4. Does David's statement, "All the days ordained for me were written in your book before one of them came to be" bring you any comfort or encouragement? Why?

If the Bible clearly states our worth to God, why do women look elsewhere for validation? Society misleads us into thinking that our self-esteem is based on our physical appearance. Some think it can come through the status we have in our communities. The positions we hold at work or in the church give us a sense of accomplishment, but can we rely on these things for our self-esteem? Society also says that pleasing personalities are an indication of our self-worth. If we rely on our appearance, where is your identity when your muscles begin to sag and wrinkles show up? When our identity is connected to our children, and they come to a place where they don't require our assistance all the time, where does that leave us? When it is directly tied to our career or job, what happens when we retire or lose that job?

I read an interesting book not long ago entitled *Becoming a Woman of Extraordinary Faith*. Author Julie Clinton quotes Blaise Pascal, "Not only do we not know God except through Jesus Christ, but also we do not know ourselves except through Jesus Christ." Our identity should be based on a concept of God's grace. We can't earn that grace; it's a gift (Ephesians 2:8)! Because of Jesus' death we are healed and have His protection. We read in 1 Peter 2:24 about the healing only God can provide. Psalm 91 was one of my father's favorite passages in the Old Testament. It speaks about God's protection, "Under His wings shall you trust and find refuge" (v. 4 AMP). Grace and peace are ours "from God our Father and from the Lord Jesus Christ" (Ephesians 1:2 AMP). Our lives in Christ can be full because God gives us everything we need (Philippians 4:19). And what about that wonderful gift of forgiveness? While we have difficulty in forgiving others, God forgives our sins on a daily basis (1 John 1:9). Yes, life in Christ increases our enjoyment to outrageous proportions. Life lived in Christ, lived to its full limits enables us to see the Master Creator for who He really is. This reminds me of a found object story. To start, I should mention that I love to find bargains. A garage sale sign causes my heart to beat faster. An estate or tag sale gives me palpitations. I love those television reality shows about friends who travel across the United States picking through barns, outbuildings, and piles of discarded junk. The saying, "One man's trash is another man's treasure" is my motto!

When my family and I lived in Denver, Colorado, one of my favorite weekend activities was to get out the newspaper's classified section to see if there were any estate sales. I would circle the ones that looked interesting and my husband would create a route. The children were old enough to be left alone for the morning, so we'd head out the door early enough to be at the prime sale before the doors opened. Our children had no desire to stand in lines waiting to traipse through dusty old houses and rummage through cardboard boxes, but my husband usually was willing to go along with me.

One Saturday we headed out first thing in the morning and drove to an older section of Denver for an estate sale. Located near the oldest part of downtown Denver, I could feel in my heart that this would be a profitable "pick." The old house wasn't very large, but when my eyes lighted on a mahogany plant stand, I knew I was in a good place! I put my name on the stand and proceeded to check out the other rooms and the collections of stuff they held. Just as I had decided that the plant stand was all I would purchase, I noticed a closet door in the dining room ajar. Since its door was open, I peeked inside in search of one more treasure. When my eyes adjusted to the dark interior, I saw a curved piece of wood leaning against the wall. It was about 28 inches long and at its widest point almost 12 inches tall.

Looking over my shoulder to make sure I wasn't breaking any estate "rules," I pulled the piece out. It was dark, dark brown, not especially pretty, but its shape was interesting. I turned around and asked one of the salespersons if it was for sale. "One dollar, and it's yours," she said. That's all I needed to hear. My husband had learned not to question my purchase choices, so we paid for the board and plant stand and went on our way.

Several days later, armed with paint remover, I prepared a patio table for my operation. I lathered the paint-removing chemical all over the piece of wood and went inside to wait the proper amount of time for it to work its magic. When I returned outside about 20 minutes later, I began to shout, "Come and see! See what I've got!" Used to my excitement over treasure buys, my family reluctantly gathered to see Mom's latest find. What they saw this time, however, caused their eyes to open wider. This time, I really had gotten a treasure—an unexpected work of art, a special piece.

Buried under years of grime and brown paint, a woodcarving had emerged. Probably the top of an old dresser, the transformed piece was covered with intricately carved oak leaves and acorns. Gone was the ugly brown piece of wood and in its place was a beautiful carving in golden oak. Once I removed all of the brown paint and sealed the surface, I mounted the carved piece above the inside of our home's front door. Since 1984, this piece of wood is one of the first things placed in our new homes. We have moved seven times since then, and this special treasure has been a symbol for home in three states. Whether we have rented, owned, or been mobile-home-park residents, it has been the symbol that says, "This is our home." It was one of the first things I unpacked in our new place this year, and it now rests in its customary location over the front door. This found object has witnessed many family occasions. It has been privy to discussions about our futures and how God has worked in our individual and family lives. An ordinary piece of wood turned into something extraordinary by a skilled carver. This artwork reminds me that a found object doesn't necessarily have to be anything valuable to anyone but its finder.

A found object doesn't have to be beautiful either. The worth of a found object is strictly in the eye of the beholder.

When I think back to my experience of finding that piece of ugly-looking wood, I remember the look of disbelief in my husband's eyes when I claimed it for my own. A dollar

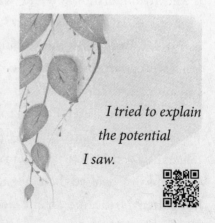

I tried to explain the potential I saw.

was too much as far as he was concerned. If I had tried to explain to him the potential I saw, he would never have believed me because he saw the grime, dirt, and paint.

At times, when God speaks to us and tells us about His direction for our lives, we refuse to see the potential in our lives or in our circumstances. We fail to comprehend what His power can accomplish. When God sends someone into our lives with a message or insight, or touches us through His Word, we don't always grasp the full meaning of what He wants us to see or do. There have been many times in my life that I have had a word from God and have failed to realize its importance or the impact it could have on my life. All of us have had similar experiences if we have honestly sought God's will and direction for our lives. As Paul says in 1 Corinthians 13:12, "For now we see through a glass, darkly; but then face to face: now I know in part; but then shall I know even as also I am known."

When we joined a large church in a Denver suburb in the 1980s, I was asked to serve temporarily as the preschool director. Little did I know that I would hold that position for two years, two months, and two days! I was faced with managing 13 preschool departments; hiring paid staff; enlisting, training, and working with more than 200 volunteers, as well as providing age-level training for Bible study teachers.

As I slowly began to sift through my varied responsibilities, I realized that God had actually prepared me for the job for many years. I had been a preschool missions leader; the Vacation Bible

School director for a church which enrolled 350 children one year; led church projects, committees, outreach work; helped to establish a Christian school; and led training seminars for teachers and missions leaders. In the midst of these activities and during different times, I owned two small businesses.

As the Colorado church's new preschool director, I did these same tasks. If God had told me a dozen years before that I would be using all the skills I had learned, I would probably have laughed and not believed Him like Sarah did in the Old Testament when God told her she would have a baby when she was over 90!

My "temporary" status as preschool director was a time of many blessings. God called others to work alongside me, and we saw the preschool ministry grow—both in numbers and purpose. We took teacher preparation seriously and made strong progress toward teaching preschoolers about God and His love for the world. Families began to see the importance of instilling this love in their little ones as we provided opportunities for their children to learn about missionaries and how God wanted them to tell others about His Son Jesus.

I haven't listed the things I've been able to do with and for God to impress you! I want you to see the variety of ways God uses our abilities and availability when we understand how much He loves us and wants the best for us. I try never to take any experience for granted, knowing that God has a master plan and can use anything I learn in the future for a larger purpose. Would I trade anything for those years of service or the blessings I received working with/ for preschoolers? Absolutely not! Did those early years prepare me for further service? That's another yes!

Just like my wooden, carved found object, my life has been carved by a Master. The intricate makeup of my personality and my God-given abilities have come together and have, at times, been pleasing to God. As a work of art, I need to choose to do His work, serve as He directs, and be where He asks me to be. Just as I believed there was hidden potential in that ugly piece of wood I got that day, God sees in me potential for unusual service. It is my responsibility to be available and alert to His guidance. My self-esteem needs to continue to become healthier so I am confident to live the call He has placed on my life.

Zig Ziglar summed it up beautifully when he talked about how we let our sense of shame overcome us and feelings of worthless-ness and hopelessness debilitate us, "We are wonderfully created, tragically fallen, deeply loved, and completely forgiven."

Before you move on to the next chapter and its story, take a few minutes to think about factors that influence your self-esteem.

Using a scale of 1–10, score your self-esteem as it relates to the following:

_____ physical features   _____ intelligence

_____ expertise   _____ achievements

_____ talents   _____ social connections

_____ job/career   _____ financial status

_____ easy to like   _____ attributes/ character traits

_____ life roles   _____ confidence

Found Treasure

ON TARGET

God knows me and still accepts me.
Because of this, I can accept myself.
God knows me and still loves me.
Because of this, I can love myself.
God knows me and still gives me esteem.
Because of this, I can give esteem to myself.

WHAT DO YOU THINK WHEN YOU READ SOMETHING like this? Do you immediately begin to react by saying something like, "That's OK for so-and-so, but it doesn't help me at all"? Do you discount the statements because you believe you are the exception? How you answer these questions, and how you respond to the statements above gives insight into how healthy your self-esteem is.

Here's another question: what things come to your mind when the term *self-esteem* is used in any context? Can you make a list of issues that are involved in a woman's idea about who she is? Here are a few I listed that can determine how a woman feels about herself:

- VIEW OF FEMININITY—a woman's general approach to her abilities and place in society
- PHYSICAL APPEARANCE—issues relating to age, addictions, weight, etc.
- EMOTIONAL HEALTH—presence of physical, verbal, emotional abuse
- STATUS—education, professional positions, achievements
- RELATIONSHIPS—family, church, workplace

That's a long list, isn't it? We could spend a lot of time on each of these issues. (Note: If one in particular touches you, visit your local library or Christian bookstore and search for a credible source. Notice I said "credible!" For every resource that is well-written by a thoughtful author, there are two others that will distract you from finding biblically based information. Be discerning in your search.)

Is your list of self-esteem issues as long as mine? You probably thought of some things I missed. I think if we concentrate on topics in general categories, we will gain some new insights along the way, and perhaps finish in this decade!

So, with our lists in hand—or on your laptop, tablet, smartphone, or wherever—what is the best way to move toward a healthier self-esteem? The Bible passages I mentioned in chapter 1 (p. 17) will help you understand how much God values you and that He has a special plan for your life. As an adult, I have always subscribed to the belief that as God shows us what to do, it is our responsibility to act. No one can do this for us. We may need to change harmful thought patterns that we have developed over the years. We need to understand that God will provide for us as we work to leave hurtful incidents behind.

I called this chapter "On Target" because of an experience I had several years ago. As I look back on my first missions trip, I see that God's hand directed each of us on the team. We were able to do what we did because our individual self-esteems were healthy enough to attempt what He challenged us to do. Here's what happened.

Several years ago our statewide women's missions organization formalized a partnership with Croatian Baptist women. It was something new for us because we had always been on the receiving end of help, and now we were making our first attempt to help women grow as leaders and to develop a women's missions organization in another country. After several months of investigation and planning, we sent our first short-term missions team to this Eastern European nation.

During the preparation time for our trip, we began to learn about Croatia. Our team leader knew that our historical knowledge would give us insights into the women with whom we would be working. Many of the women we would meet had lost family members during the civil war that ravaged the country for almost ten years. Many of the Croatian women had been evacuated from their homes during the war, or their homes had been destroyed. We were to see proof of bombings and gunfire as we took brief tours of the areas surrounding the towns where we stayed while in Croatia. The walls of many houses and public buildings were pockmarked with holes from the shelling. The Christian women who would attend our leadership workshops were slowly healing from the effects of long-term hostilities between ethnic factions. They had come to the point that they didn't want to be separated by hatred, fear, and prejudice any longer.

The day of our departure arrived, and two of us met at the Los Angeles International Airport for the first leg of our trip. Because we were new at long-distance traveling, we decided to do it all at once. Lesson learned! The third member from our state had sense enough to break up her trip. We have photographs showing how excited we were leaving when ready to leave, but we don't show anyone how we looked when we got back home. We had carefully planned the workshops we would be leading. We had divided the responsibilities and had thoughtfully considered what we had been told the Croatian women needed.

When we arrived in the capital city of Zagreb, we were met by the Croatian Baptist Union's president and his wife, who was serving as the president of the women's programs. She explained that as the country emerged from years of civil war, the women were just beginning to feel God's call on their lives and were answering that call. They wanted to learn how they could do missions and what it could look like in their part of the world. Our week in Croatia had been planned almost down to the minute, with several women's events. One large meeting was for all the women. It was held in Cakovec. When we arrived, we were housed at the Cow Farm, a dairy that had been established after the war to provide employment in the terribly depressed Croatian economy.

The farm was a delightful place on the outskirts of the town. We went to sleep at night to the sounds of mooing cows and awoke in the morning to their movements out to pasture. The accommodations were surprisingly modern, and the cook enlisted to provide some of our meals prepared some delicious treats for us. Using the farm as our base, we launched into the culture and sights of the area.

As the day for the national event approached, we toured the huge facility that had been built as the result of a visionary's dream. Construction on the ministry center was almost completed. It contained dormitory rooms for orphaned boys, a partially finished Internet café, and an auditorium that would seat 900 easily. As we took the tour, we felt the burden of our influence on women whose opinions had never been asked, women who were beginning to see God's moving in their lives.

The day finally arrived and we were in our assigned places. Following a time of worship, the women were told what workshops were being offered by Americans. When it was time to break up into smaller groups, the majority of the women remained in their seats. The announcement was made again, and the women were encouraged to move to the designated locations for the workshops. Still, they sat. They had never been given the opportunity to learn this way; in fact, many had never attended a workshop or a breakout session. The pressure was on to deliver pertinent and applicable information!

God had put our team together to meet the needs of the Croatian women that day. The fledgling Croatian leadership team had requested a team comprised of both young and older women— we ranged in age from early 30s to 70-plus. They had asked for ethnic diversity—our team had African American, Latino, and EuroAmerican women on it. Their optimal team would include both working women and stay-at-home women—our team had a pastor's wife, a denominational employee, a single woman, one retired woman, and a young mother. God accomplishes far more than we could ever dream of putting together on our own. As we began to lead our workshops, it was immediately apparent that we were in the right place at the right time doing what God wanted us to do.

After our initial tour of the large facility, we went outside to the front of the building to have our photograph taken. As we stood in the shade for a few minutes, we took photos of the tower that had been designed to represent a hand lifting up toward heaven and of the steps leading to the front entrance. We stood in a rocked planter bed of small rocks in the shade, and as we waited, I began to look more closely at the rocks. One small rock caught my eye and I stooped to pick it up. A found object! I believe it was a granite rock with white, gray, and dark gray color gradations. It had a series of rings on one side that resembled a target.

As I have held this rock in my hands over the passing years, I have decided it was confirmation that I was "on target" with God's will for my life at that time. The rock reminded me of the first email about the missions trip landed in my inbox. I printed it off immediately and took it home to show to my husband. I simply handed it to him with no comment. His response? "This has got your name written all over it!" I forwarded the message to a close friend, again with no comment. I received an immediate response complete with exclamation points. "This is for us! What do we need to do to go?" That set the entire process in motion and the result was five of us traveling 12 hours to teach women about becoming women of influence.

Jeremiah 29:13, "And ye shall seek me, and find me, when ye shall search for me with all your heart" has been used by many to affirm God's direction in their lives. This verse directed me that year to Croatia, where the experiences I had will remain with me for the rest of my life. Being on target for God begins with seeking

His direction. That seeking requires us to have open minds and flexible spirits. It will demand our faithfulness to carry out whatever He instructs us to do even though we may not fully understand the whys.

If our self-esteem is unhealthy, it is easy to engage in faulty reasoning. We may come to the conclusion that God can't use us because we aren't capable or worthy of being used. Being on target necessitates action. It is not enough to merely seek God's will, to be flexible, or to understand all the details. It is our job to follow through with some type of action as He directs. Will we have all the answers, all the solutions? Probably not, but we must still take steps to acknowledge God's direction for us.

As we searched for God's will for our team, we agreed that the one quality we would need to display the most would be flexibility. We know this, but actually being flexible is not always easy. Anyone who has participated in an overseas missions trip will tell you that flexibility is a critical element. You may have to throw all your plans out the window. Our flexibility was tested numerous times and I believe we rolled with the punches most of the time. One specific incident comes to my mind: It was unusual for a woman to speak in public in Croatia, so we were delighted when our team leader was asked to bring a brief message at an evening worship service on the day of the large women's gathering. We were delighted, but she didn't share our enthusiasm. She hadn't been told about this ahead of time. Nowhere did it appear on our team's to-do list. She rallied to the occasion, and we were all proud of her as she let God use her in this unique way.

We saw evidence of being on target by our presence in Croatia when we had a women's gathering right before we left the country. The meeting was held in a church in Karlovac which had been the frontline during Croatia's civil war. The church's pastor and wife had remained in the city despite the fighting all around them. They became a lighthouse for Christ during the long siege on the city. The pastor's wife introduced each of us and asked us to say something in farewell. Then the Croatian women were asked to share their impression of the weeklong meetings. As the translators put their comments into English, I looked across the room at my close friend. She, too, had tears in her eyes as one woman said, "We knew what we needed to do. We have known about missions. You have given us wings to fly!"

My target rock is a special, treasured found object that will always remind me that I should keep seeking God's direction for my movements on a daily basis. If I am on target, I will become aware of ministry opportunities. Being on target will mean that I will realize that life's interruptions are divine appointments for me. My self-esteem plays a critical role in whether I listen when God calls me. As confidence in my abilities grows, I will be able to truly be on target for Him.

Lord, help me understand that it is not enough to see the opportunity for ministry but that I must see Your hand moving, be flexible, and take action!

Quite a story, right? I hope you were able to read between the lines and hear all the things I didn't describe. There were many frustrations, and we were nervous a lot of the time. That was overshadowed, however, by the understanding that if God directs us to do something, He goes before us. I used to work with a gentleman who frequently said, "God pays for what He orders." Isn't that great? And, it's true!

To sum up what we've talked about in this chapter, remember these things:

- We can't dwell on how sinful we are and how unworthy we are.
- When we experience God's grace and see the beauty and wonder of who we are in Christ, we will come to love ourselves.
- We can love how we look because we know life is deeper than our skin's surface.
- We can delight in our talents, gifts, and resources.

The Message phrases Psalm 19:7−9 this way:

> The revelation of GOD is whole and pulls our lives together. The signposts of GOD are clear and point out the right road. The life-maps of GOD are right, showing the way to joy. The directions of GOD are plain and easy on the eyes. GOD's reputation is twenty-four-carat gold, with a lifetime guarantee. The decisions of GOD are accurate down to the nth degree.

When a woman accepts Jesus, God transforms her life. He covers her with His grace. He covers her with His infinite love. He covers her with His mercy. And her self-esteem grows!

Take a few minutes to think about factors that influence your self-esteem. Look at your own list and then using a scale of 1–10, score where you put your sense of self-esteem:

____ physical features   ____ intelligence

____ expertise   ____ achievements

____ talents   ____ social connections

____ job/career   ____ financial status

____ likability   ____ attributes/character traits

____ roles as mother, wife, etc.   ____ confidence

Found Treasure

DOLLAR WISE

LIVING IN THE WEST MOST OF MY ADULT LIFE, I HAVE always had access to beaches. While I thought it enjoyable to drive to the shore, I was not a frequent visitor of the surf and sand. Until, sometime between the years when my children were in high school and after they had all left home, I became passionate about listening to the sounds of the surf. I still don't know exactly when it happened or what caused it but at some point I developed an intense desire to be at the beach.

Because my job required me to be all over the state where I lived, I began to plan my routes based on how many beaches I could visit. I would tell my husband the schedule for the week and either preface or summarize my comments by asking, "Is there a beach on the way there or near there?" We made it a habit to carry low beach chairs, beach towels, and an umbrella. My storage shed had an entire shelf dedicated to beach paraphernalia!

Weather had no bearing on my desire for the ebb and flow of waves. I preferred hot sun that warmed the sand so that its heat soaked through my beach towel into my bones. Clouds that obscured the sun were also fine with me. I liked a calm day with just a gentle breeze, but if the wind was howling, I could handle it because I could see the waves and dig my feet into the sand. Suffice it to say that I'm a beach gal who has never seen a beach she doesn't love!

I am not a surfer or a swimmer. I don't snorkel or wind sail. When I'm on a beach, all I need is a chair of some type, a towel, and something to read. I have conducted a lot of business while at the beach, even making calls and taking messages. I was the prototype for the television commercial about the mom whose children complained because she was always working. In the commercial's ministory she sets everything aside to spend the day at the beach with her children. My office traveled with me, but that didn't bother me *if* I were on a beach somewhere.

One week several years ago, I was determined to spend some quality time at the beach between meetings. The day was a cloudy one, the wind was blowing, and it was not beach season. Nothing was going to deter me, however, so we found a parking place near access to the sand. It was chilly, so my husband elected to stay in the car. I put on a hooded sweatshirt, zipped it all the way up to my chin, and was ready for whatever the beach could offer. Little did I know what it was offering that day! The wind was blowing too hard to try to read, so I abandoned that idea. I left my cell phone in the car because I wouldn't have been able to carry on a conversation amidst the sounds of roaring wind and because of the howling winds and the crashing waves. So, heading into the stiff wind, I made my way to the steps going down to the sand. At the top of the stairs I met a young boy coming up who was very excited to show his mother something in his hand. I couldn't help looking to see what was so interesting. He looked up at me and thrust out his hand so I could see saying, "You can have this one if you'd like." A beautiful, perfectly formed sand dollar rested in the palm of his hand.

When I asked where he had found his treasure, he gestured out toward the surf and swept his arm back and forth. "They are all over the sand! They washed up during the night, I guess." I thanked the boy for his offer and assured him I would go down to see if I could find my own dollars. With the wind whipping my hair around my face and the cold stinging my skin, I pulled the hood tighter and started off on my own treasure hunt. At first I didn't see a single thing out of the ordinary. I walked several yards with my head down (blessed relief from the wind) and looked carefully for the fragile, round disks. Before too long I was rewarded by finding the first dollar. It was chipped, though, and I let it fall out of my hand. Another dollar was rejected and another. Then, there it was. The first whole sand dollar I'd ever found!

I continued walking down the shore into the strong wind. My hands were cold; so were my face and nose. I realized, however, that this was an unusual opportunity. I would probably never have the chance to gather sand dollars this way again because it was so unusual to find so many in one place. The young boy's enthusiasm was catching as I found dollar after dollar in the sand that day. The dollars varied in color and size, but all of them were beautiful.

Sand dollars are spiny-skinned creatures that prefer the muddy, soft bottom areas of the ocean. When alive they are dark in color and are covered with short, dark spines that look almost like fur. Their spines enable them to move around on the sea bottom and to pull small pieces of food into their mouths. Sand dollars are also called "sand cakes" and "cake urchins." In South Africa they are called "pansy shells" because of the five petals on the top resembling a garden flower. Finding sand dollars that are whitish in color on the shore is an indication that the urchins are no longer alive. When I returned home after my business trip, I washed all my dollars and set them out in the sun to bleach. As I laid out about 20 sand dollars in a shallow tray, I was overcome by a sense of wonder. I couldn't help but think about the beauty of these creations. God had indeed made something of great beauty when sand dollars came into His mind. His creation had become a found object for me.

Like the sand dollars I collected, each of us is a unique creation. No two of us alike. Our existence, just like the sand dollar, is to glorify God. We have been designed to proclaim His majesty and power. As the psalmist says in Psalm 107:24 (NIV), "They saw the works of the LORD, his wonderful deeds in the deep."

I have stored my found objects to protect them from breakage. We, however, do not have the luxury of being wrapped and stored away on a shelf. God created us for His purpose and use.

On the contrary, God's glory is not proclaimed by anything sitting on a shelf, unavailable, kept for later use. Just as I wrapped up my sand dollars and put them away for safe keeping, we make the decision about whether we will be available to be used by God.

What influences that decision? Our attitudes toward service is one factor. If I believe that only those called into full-time ministry are to serve God, I have put myself on the shelf. Galatians 5:13 tells us that we have been called to God in a variety of ways. "For, brethren, ye have been called into liberty; only use not liberty for an occasion to the flesh, but by love serve one another."

The abilities I have should be used for God's kingdom's work. The networks I form can be connecting points to God and His love. I will never be perfectly equipped to do God's will and to answer His call on my life, but as I work on having a positive attitude toward service, I will move off the shelf into the blessings only service can bring. My being available demonstrates that I regard service as a personal mandate.

Another factor in making a decision to be available to God is an understanding of the impact my service can have. The ultimate purpose of working for and with God in our world is to see persons, families, communities, and nations come to a saving knowledge of Jesus: "Give praise to the LORD, proclaim his name; make known among the nations what he has done" (Psalm 105:1 NIV). Our service comes in many forms. I use my abilities and interests in ways that may be completely opposite of your approach to service.

How have I used my interests and abilities in service? My interest in children has led me to work with missions groups for preschoolers, participate in Vacation Bible School, and teach parents how to involve their families in missions. I love to crochet and that interest motivated me to make hair ties for missions volunteers to give to little girls in Brazil as they learned about Jesus. Now, winter nights will find me crocheting baby blankets for women in crisis shelters and centers. All of us can connect ordinary interests and skills to ministry opportunities.

Will I ever meet those Brazilian girls or those new moms who visit the shelter? Probably not. But, the love I have for others is translated into action to meet needs. I help plant God's love in others' lives.

The third thing we must understand is the part our self-esteem plays in using our abilities for God. We must assess our abilities and then prepare ourselves to use those abilities for Him. If our self-esteem is not healthy, our effectiveness for God will be limited. If this is true, and I believe it is, we need to make an effort to understand ourselves. That cold, blustery day on the beach is a fond memory for me. I don't remember which beach I visited but I remember the outcome! I finally had to leave because I was so cold. I took treasures with me, though. My found objects have moved with me and are still in a safe place. They are on the shelf, so to speak, but I am continuing to discover ways to serve God so that "whether therefore ye eat, or drink, or whatsoever ye do, do all to the glory of God" (1 Corinthians 10:31).

Have you ever been in a situation where you felt as if you'd been transplanted into a foreign environment? You were flailing around, ready to sink under the pressure to perform in an area where you had no expertise. You'd been asked to do something that was way beyond your confidence level. You were really out of your comfort zone!

A key element in a healthy self-esteem is the ability to understand yourself. You might have just said, "Well, of course. What is she talking about? Everyone knows themselves!" Oh really? Are you certain that is true? When you find yourself—to use a fishing term—*floundering* in some circumstance at work or in your home, can you explain your actions? We may not let everyone around us know that we are struggling inside to accomplish an assignment or maintain our equilibrium. All the internal faltering is hidden, but it takes its toll on our confidence.

When we finally weather the difficulty, we realize that some of our actions have been mysterious to us. We shake our heads and wonder, *Why in the world did I do that? How could I have said that?* Many actions arise from how we view ourselves. If our self-image is a poor one, our struggles will be deep ones most likely affecting multiple areas of our lives. Low self-esteem—due, in part to a lack of self-understanding—dictates our responses in the workplace, at home, at church, and even with our friends and neighbors.

Let's take a simple example. What does society tell us about our appearance? We all need to be thin (I'm feeling bad already!). Our teeth must be white and straight. Whether we look good with long hair or not, the ultimate is to have long, shiny hair with absolutely no gray. Oh! And we are to be completely balanced "doing it all." I don't know about you, but I'm feeling guilty that I haven't achieved perfection!

What if we are not professional, oh-so-thin models, with straight teeth and long hair living in balance—is there hope for us? Do we all have to achieve our culture's ideal looks? Think a little about famous people throughout history who have been less than perfect by society's standard. History recorded that the Greek orator Demosthenes had a speech impairment. Julius Caesar had epilepsy. George Washington sported horrible false teeth. Have you looked at a photograph of Abraham Lincoln lately? Franklin Delano Roosevelt spent most of his adult life in a wheelchair. Neither Eleanor Roosevelt, Golda Meir, Mary McLeod Bethune, or Mother Teresa might have made it to the fashion runway, Luciano Pavarotti was rotund. And what about Jimmy Durante's classic nose?!

No, "perfection" in our appearance, nor public poise are the basis for healthy self-esteem. Should we strive to look *our* best? Of course! Should we learn to function in various situations and be focused and prepared? Yes, but we need to view ourselves through *God's* eyes. We know He values us, but is that simply as part of humanity? Or does His interest go deeper?

In Grady Nutt's book, entitled *Being Me*, he stresses that when we learn to be ourselves, we will fulfill God's plan for our lives. We get ourselves into a lot of trouble when we compare ourselves to someone else and the path God has chosen for them. We begin to think, *Now why couldn't I do that? Wait a minute. I never could do that!* And we are defeated. By not listening to God, understanding ourselves, and then moving forward, we limit how He can work in and through us. Answer the following questions. Your answers to these questions may give you some ideas about why your self-esteem isn't as healthy as it can be.

- Are you a masterpiece? Read Ephesians 2:10.
- Are you unique? Look up Genesis 1:27.
- Are you a robot or do you have dignity with free will? Read Proverbs 16:9.
- What did Jesus do to demonstrate His desire to have a relationship with us? Read 1 Peter 1:18–20.

We have all met women who don't seem to see that they have any worth at all. We shake our heads and wonder why they don't do something about their attitude. What a woman believes about herself radically affects the way she lives, the goals she makes, the heights of character she aspires to, the way she relates to people, and how she connects to God. See what you think about these statements about how self-esteem develops:

> "No one can make you feel inferior unless you allow them to." —*Eleanor Roosevelt*

> "They cannot take away our self respect if we do not give it to them." —*Mahatma Gandhi*

> "You can't depend on your eyes when your imagination is out of focus." —*Mark Twain*

Do you agree with these ideas? Should we let others dictate what we do or don't do? Should we give others power over us which determines how we value ourselves? Are things out of focus, as Twain said, keeping us from understanding what our abilities are? If an element of our self-esteem stems from what others tell us, either their advice or criticism, what can we do to foster understanding our worth?

I'm a bottom line kind of woman, always searching for a practical solution, and I have discovered several ideas or remedies I believe might help you as you search for and work toward a healthier understanding of yourself. Here are four of them:

1. *Thank God that He created you.* We need to remember that God made us in His image (Genesis 1:27) and that He was pleased with what He did. Who are we to negate that creativity?

2. *Try every day to demonstrate the real you, the God-created you, to your family and friends.* Those hardest to please are our families and friends. But are we to live life trying to please them or God? God wants us to excel at being who He created us to be.

3. *Accept how God has made you and learn to be a friend to yourself.* We are often our own harshest critic! We second-guess our decisions, demean our accomplishments, and belittle all that we do.

4. *Resist pressure to do things that don't match who you know you are.* Women have a lot of pressure in their lives! Pressure to perform, pressure to balance everything, pressure to look "just right," pressure to be everything to everyone. Our actions need to demonstrate that we are living and working within who we truly are.

How important is acceptance in our lives?

Picture this: The class let out for recess, and all the kids ran out to the playground. The boys headed for the balls, and the girls clustered near the fence to chatter. Soon there are four or five groups of little girls, leaning forward to hear each other's whispers. Off to one side, three girls stand alone. Dressed like the others, they, however, don't have a group. They stand uncertainly, waiting for what seems an interminable time, for the bell to ring signaling the end of recess. These girls don't fit. For some reason, they have been excluded from the lively chatter and excited squeals of the small groups. They have not been accepted into the "inner circles" of the fifth grade.

This scenario happens everywhere, every day. The scene morphs some during middle school and high school, but there are always those girls who are not part of the friendships that develop around common activities and interests. As females reach adulthood, they still seek acceptance on many levels as their abilities, preferences, and personalities dictate their behavior.

When a girl or woman accepts Jesus as her Savior, she continues her lifetime journey toward self-acceptance. The healthy images we are born with become distorted through the years because we try to mold them into what we think others demand. We live our lives trying to fit into roles dictated by others. For years, my father and my one brother took an annual camping trip. It was, after all, what fathers and sons did to bond, right? One year, my brother ventured to tell Daddy, "You know, I don't care if we go camping this year. I don't really like camping very much." His comment took my father completely by surprise, who responded, "Wow! I always went because I thought you enjoyed it! I've never liked camping either!"

I don't think we ever lose our desire to be accepted. We certainly spend a lot of time seeking it, don't we? I believe we must come to a point in our lives when we set aside the emphasis of society, we need to rely on God to direct our movements and mold our personalities into what is acceptable in His eyes. Only then will we achieve the acceptance that matters. Because of our acceptance of Christ's sacrifice, His Father accepted us.

Chapter 3

What about my life circumstances?

As you've been reading, you may have thought, *Wait a sec, my circumstances are different! How am I supposed to have a healthy self-esteem when life has undermined me?* Do life circumstances really affect our self-esteem? Of course they do! Is there nothing we can do to remedy this? Yes, I believe there is. Let's look at two life circumstances that will impact most of us.

First, aging is an issue. Unless we go home to be with Jesus before wrinkles appear, most of us will face not only what we see in the mirror as we turn sideways trying to find our waist but also we will feel the effects of our age "numbers" on our self-esteem.. Some cultures bestow dignity and status on older members. American culture isn't noted for this; older adults are often described as "over the hill" or "out of it." Aging can bring isolation, emotional problems, and the ever-present physical issues. Does reaching some number automatically erase wisdom? Or diminish expertise? In most cases, the answer is no!

If you are reading this book and are an older adult, life is definitely not over! One phase has probably ended, but life hasn't. In a moment of frustration over this issue several months ago, I wrote a musing, as I like to call it, in which I vented about aging. I reread it last week and for the most part, I still feel the same! As we age, we must continue to seek God's face and His perfect will for our continued (albeit changed) service for Him. There is a place for everyone in His plan; our responsibility is to rely on Him to reveal what and where it is.

A second area that impacts many women is that of being widowed or divorced. Statistics change every year, but both of these life circumstances can undermine a woman's self-esteem. Women are faced with learning to do things they have never done before such as handling important household business, providing for children, and being newly single. They may struggle with financial issues no one prepared them for. Not only are they alone, part of their identity was linked to their husband. I met a woman whose husband was in full-time ministry and died suddenly. She told me that she lost a large part of her identity when he died. She struggled to find a personal ministry and to develop skills that would carry her through the difficult period of adjustment.

Divorce statistics reveal that Christ followers divorce at almost the same rate as anyone else. That's a sad statistic, but it's a difficult reality many women must face. Many of the same issues arise. Women don't prepare for divorce. I've never seen a college course offered on the subject! In the midst of emotional highs and basement lows, a woman faces financial uncertainty and rebuilding a new life without a helpmate.

How do these two circumstances affect women? In addition to the devastation of a failed relationship, there is a loss of identity and most likely, a loss of self-esteem. Everyone will have an opinion about what you should do. You realize that, don't you? The questions will come: How in the world will you survive? Whose advice do you follow? How do you please everyone? Michele Halseide, in *Words to Live by for Women*, said, "We will never grow in our relationship with God if we don't have the gumption to become single-minded, bent on pleasing God—and only God."

Is what she said based on the truth of Scripture? Read 1 Thessalonians 4:1. What do you think? If we want to build a healthy self-esteem, we need to make the effort to understand ourselves. That understanding will enable us to live in a way that pleases God and moves us toward His plan. I'm afraid that many times as I move through my days, I am like the person a friend of mine describes in her poem "Caught in the Game" (Madelyn Keach. Used by permission.).

We need to live for the line, not the dot, believing that God has placed eternity in our hearts and that the only way to satisfy the longing connected with that reality is to be in relationship with him. From this relationship with God, we will be empowered to conquer discontent and find strength to live with a perspective and priorities that run counter to our culture.

Like a chameleon, we move, swift and slow, changing colors as we go. We don coats of many colors to survive, pretend and stalk our prey. The color of righteousness blinds us to compassion. The color of generosity disguises our greed. We move through life camouflaged, busy changing colors we are captured by our own deceit. Truth breathes our name, urging, calling, but we choose to play the game!

"It is not a question of whether you can be somebody.
You ARE somebody."

—*Joel Wells*

Found Treasure

CHAPTER 4

MEANT FOR YOU

ONE OF THE MOST REWARDING RELATIONSHIPS IN MY life has been with a woman who mentored me both spiritually and professionally. We met at a national women's missions training event and established a long-lasting friendship. Her work as an early childhood development specialist prepared her for a leadership role for the national women's missions organization.

Through a series of circumstances over a period of years, Ethel and I met again when she came to my state as a missions volunteer. Her years of experience made her an expert not only in organizational issues but also as a professional woman. Her experiences in the early years of her career happened when most women did not work outside their homes. They gave her a different perspective that enabled her to help other women to move forward in their leadership roles.

When I assumed the state denominational position, Ethel had been serving as the interim leader. She was ready to return home, but I let her know immediately that she couldn't leave yet! I needed her input and understanding that couldn't be found in any personnel manual or training leaflet. She graciously agreed to stay a few more weeks until I felt comfortable with all that was involved in this new role. Her assistance during those days formed a bond between us that still exists today.

A strong mentoring relationship may change over time, and that's what happened to ours. When Ethel decided most of her long-distance traveling days were over, she mentored me from a distance. We had long conversations via telephone and email. We brainstormed about women's work and how to make missions exciting. Because I made an annual trip to her state, I always stayed with Ethel. We had wonderful times together as she continued to mentor me professionally.

One time Ethel and I were emailing back and forth, and I suggested that we take a road trip together. Where could we find warmth in January? How about Florida? The Florida beaches were calling our names! I decided to respond to an invitation to speak at a women's retreat in Florida.

What's not to like about winter days in the Sunshine State? We took our time driving down and enjoyed several tourist attractions along the way. It was nice not to have a strict time schedule and to enjoy long hours of conversation. We arrived in the small town on the gulf side the day before the one-day women's retreat. We were scheduled to have a session together, then lunch and a final time together. There were about 30 women present, and everyone seemed to enjoy a relaxed time, complete with door prizes.

In between lunch and the last general session, a middle-aged woman came up to me. As we talked, it became apparent that she had experienced some difficult times in her life. She was seeking companionship and an encouraging word from another woman. Just before we began a time of music, she reached out her hand to me and said, "Here, this is for you." In her hand she held a pewter ring with the inscription *God loves you* on it. Startled, I tried to refuse her gift as graciously as I could. "Oh no, you don't understand—God told me to give it to you." Evidently while I was speaking, she was touched by something that I said. Hopefully, it was God speaking through me.

The ring doesn't fit any of my fingers so I wear it on my right thumb. While it isn't valuable and probably strictly speaking is not a found object, it's certainly a treasured one! I keep it in my jewelry box as a reminder of an important lesson I learned that day: we never fully realize the impact our words have on others. I've studied about communication, but I often go through my days failing to see how what I say and how I say it influences my family, acquaintances, co-workers, and even strangers.

I don't know whether you have thought about how you communicate or how others' words impact your self-esteem. All of us have had experiences in which feelings of insecurity have surfaced because we have been recipients of harsh criticism, negativity, or verbal tirades for some mistake we've made. How do you feel when someone tromps all over you verbally? While we usually recognize our errors at work or home, an ugly confrontation over the matter leaves us feeling bruised and fragile.

I can still remember a ball game at recess when my sixth-grade teacher criticized me in front of the whole class for saying something he didn't like. Even years later as an adult, when I waited on him at the public library, I felt a hot flush of anger flood my face! His words were cutting and undermined my budding self-confidence. I found out later that he was dealing with a terminally ill wife at home, which may have been the root of his frustration.

But the way he talked to me still hurt in a way I haven't forgotten.

What does the Bible say about our communication?

God's Word is not silent on how we are to communicate with each other. We are to control our tongues as we relate to others, even at church! Let's look at some passages that are specific about what our speech patterns should be.

- *Ephesians 4:29–32.* *The Message* phrases it simply: "Watch the way you talk." The rest of the passage gives us a guideline for our everyday verbal encounters with others.
- *Philippians 4:8.* We are to "think on these things" as we talk to others. This passage leads me to believe that we choose to control—or not control—our conversations.
- *Proverbs 12:18.* Have you ever known anyone with a sharp tongue? Maybe you saw her this morning in the bathroom mirror! When we speak rashly, our words are like swords.
- *Ephesians 5:4* (NKJV). Paul warns us against "coarse jesting" in this verse. We can be harsh and cruel with our words and then try to cover them up by saying, "Oh, I was just teasing." As my granddaughter would say, "Seriously?" We wound others with a wicked sense of humor.
- *James 3:6* (NLT). Perhaps the best-known passage about the tongue, James tells it like it is. Our speech can be so nefarious

that it corrupts our entire body. "It can set your whole life on fire." That's pretty powerful, isn't it?

- *Proverbs 25:11.* "A word fitly spoken is like apples of gold in pictures of silver." We are instructed to be sure that our words build up rather than act as a one-person demolition crew. Our words are to be carefully chosen so that they are received as something of value—like bowls of sterling silver.

I live with a deaf man. No, Jan really is deaf! Like most other men, he has selective hearing, but his problem goes much deeper than a glazed look in his eyes when I talk about the antique set of mixing bowls I found at the local flea market. He began losing his hearing when he was 41 years old, and it's been a long, frustrating, difficult journey. As we have dealt together with increasing deafness, hearing aids, countless exams, surgery, and various other technologies through the years, we learned about the importance of clear communication.

Speaking to him as I enter the pantry isn't communication. Muttering gets me nowhere. Talking while my head is turned gets me nothing. With the help of abbreviated hand signals, a cochlear implant, and skilled lipreading, Jan and I have come to a place where our communication is successful about 50 percent of the time. That may not seem very high to you, but when you move from 2 percent to 50 percent, that's huge!

Because I have been so aware of the barriers to good communication, I believe it's critical for every woman to develop certain skills so that her self-esteem is healthy. If she is a poor communicator, she will not be confident in the workplace, relate to others successfully, or believe her input is valuable. I hope my brief discussion of three areas will pique your curiosity and cause you to think about how effective you are in each area.

LISTENING

Research indicates that we listen at only a 25 percent comprehension rate. It's a miracle that communication ever takes place! HighGain is a company that trains its clients to listen. Studies reveal that while we speak at 125–175 words per minute, we listen at rates up to 450 words per minute. In other words, we are thinking circles around the speaker! Because of this, we don't retain very much of what we hear. Actually, we retain only about 50 percent immediately after listening.

Why do you think it's so difficult to listen? I know why Jan has a hard time—he simply can't hear. However, deafness isn't usually the thing that keeps us from listening. We live in a static-filled world that distracts us. We hear cell phones ring, chirping text messages, and the whirring of office machines. Social media has put a halt to a lot of verbal communication. We text, tweet, and post rather than speak face-to-face or at least listen to a friend via telephone.

How does truly listening to another person benefit us? If we listen intentionally, turn off distractions, and focus, we may find that (1) others will feel valued because taking the time to listen to what someone else says shows them we care about their opinion and input; (2) listening increases understanding and wisdom. How many times do teenagers tell adults, "You never listen to me"? When we practice listening, muddied situations and complicated issues can be solved.

In *How to Say It for Women: Communicating with Confidence and Power Using the Language of Success*, an excellent communication resource, Phyllis Mindell recognizes five barriers to effective communication.

- *Filtering* means that for various reasons we decide not to listen. Perhaps we feel the gender or age of the speaker negates what he or she says. When a speaker's grammar is poor, his enunciation is unclear, or his language is foul, we don't listen. We filter out what bothers us, thereby not really hearing what is said.

- *Imprecision* also accounts for some failed communication. As women we often complain that our husbands don't listen to us. Now, whether that is selective hearing or the fact that they aren't interested in what we say is up for discussion. True communication doesn't take place if we don't show interest in what (or whom) we are hearing.

- A classic commercial features a woman entering a room and asks her husband, who is reading the newspaper, if the dress she's wearing makes her look fat. *Inattention* causes him to mutter, "Uh-huh." His agreement is not what she was seeking! Boredom, anxiety, priorities, interests, speaking speed can cause our minds to wander.

- It may be that the speaker and listener are mismatched. The speaker's terminology and assumptions may be *mismatched* and lead to communication failure.

- Last, communication fails simply because of our *inflexibility*. We don't want to be there so just try to get through to us! We aren't empathetic; we are disinterested. What the speaker says raises red flags from our past, and we cannot adapt to the present enough to listen to her point of view.

Here's something to think about: does any of this apply to everyday communication? Of course it does! When we talk to our spouses, we don't listen precisely, we aren't always attentive, and we can definitely refuse to be flexible. Our children turn the tables on us when they do the same things when we try to communicate with them. Our relationships with people at church are often destroyed because we build communication barriers brick by brick. If we as women are to develop healthy self-esteem, we simply must learn to be good listeners.

CRITICISM

There is a verse in the Apocrypha that says, "The blow of a whip raises a welt, but the blow of the tongue crushes bones." How true is this? A Yiddish proverb says it differently, "If you're out to beat a dog, you're sure to find a stick."

Criticism can help us improve, or it can demean and destroy. We need to avoid falling into the habit of using what I call "toxic speech." The recipients of ugly, critical words are the walking wounded. Self-esteem can be severely damaged when someone is repeatedly told they have no value and aren't capable of doing anything right. Once a woman who worked at a coffee shop I frequent asked me what I was doing while I was working on my computer. I explained I was teaching a semester class on women's self-esteem. She said, "Oh, you mean problems like he tells you over and over that you aren't worth anything?" I replied that yes, unfortunately, that happens sometimes. To this comment, she said, "Been there, done that, got rid of him! I'd like to read the book, if you ever write one about it."

There are women all around us—perhaps even some of you—whose self-esteem has been flattened by negative criticism. We can profit from positive, constructive criticism, but words spoken in anger or disdain can annihilate our self-esteem. I think you'd agree that none of us wants to be on the receiving end of those ugly words. How then, can we keep from developing that kind of critical air in our own speech with/to others? How can we stop our toxic talk? Here are a few ideas.

- Focus on the here and now rather than there and then. When we want to give feedback to someone, it's best to give it sooner than later. If we wait, there is a good chance that we will, as my mother used to say, stew about it and let it fester.

- It's often better to share ideas, not advice. Think about Job's friends. Was their advice good advice? Remember that advice is like garlic—a little goes a long way!

- Determine to keep a positive attitude. Choose to be positive instead of sinking into negativity.

- If you are critical of others, change that habit! Recall how you've felt when harsh words came your way. Remember how belittled you felt? How minimized you were? Don't do that to anyone else.

Chapter 4

PRACTICAL COMMUNICATION SKILLS

When I had carpal tunnel surgery last summer, I was very interested in what aftersurgery care would involve. I asked questions about how I would feel, when stitches would be removed, and when I could return to my normal activities. The surgery was a breeze, actually. The recovery, though it wasn't long, wasn't pleasant! My entire arm was numb for 14 hours, and I was hot due to all the bandages from elbow past my wrist.

We must realize that just as surgery requires some period of recovery afterward, there is some aftercare required communicating with others. Our words have long-term effects. The following exercise may help you at work, as you give a project report at your child's school, or during a community activity. Aim for recovery, for a more effective communication style in all areas of your life.

Write a more precise word or phrase for each of the following:

Share _____

Chat _____

Very, very important _____

As soon as possible _____

Rewrite the following words or phrases to make them sound more powerful:

I feel this product will work _____

I hope _____

I think this is about _____

I would like to _____

_____

_____

Circle the words and phrases that are good uses of body language:

Eye contact

Pointing

Standing with hands at side

Nodding

Holding head in cocked position

Natural gestures

No facial expression

So then, our daily communications with others can create a sense of well-being at the end of the day, or they can leave us with a haunting realization that we have left things unsaid, poorly stated, giving our co-workers, neighbors, family members, and friends reason to feel hurt or confused over our failure to engage in Christ-honoring conversations with them.

"The difference between the right word and the almost right word is the difference between lightning and the lightning bug."
—MARK TWAIN

As we spend a large part of our life seeking to make our opinions known and our meanings clear, we can remember that our words are "apples of gold in pictures of silver" (Proverbs 25:11). The writer of this proverb knew the importance of choosing one's words carefully. He understood that words have power. Our words can uplift, unify, encourage, and educate. They also can maim, undermine, and cause conflict.

Our everyday lives are peppered with communication, whether it reflects God's love or our own poor judgment.

Words are really not found objects. However, others' response to what we say and how we say it can bring unexpected pleasure. Some of my word choices were used by God to touch that Florida woman. Her response was to give me something of special meaning to her. I was the fortunate recipient of her listening to not only words but to God's prompting. Perhaps instead of leaving the ring in my jewelry box, I should put the treasure on a chain and wear it around my neck as a constant reminder to think about my words and speak only in love.

Found Treasure

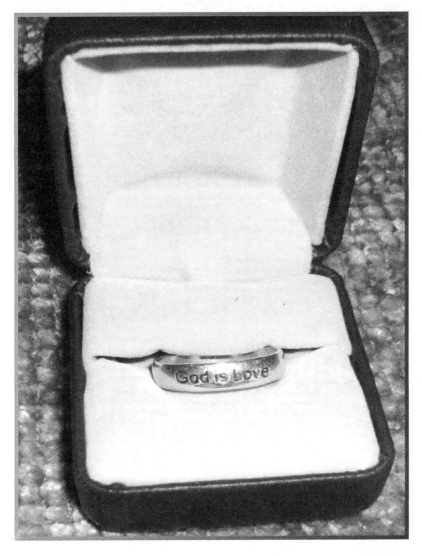

CHAPTER 5

AN UNLIKELY PLACE

HAVE YOU EVER WANTED TO JUST PULL THE BLANKET over your head and stay in bed all day? Or maybe you've thought about running away for a day—a long day—when no one calls out for help or needs you to find a lost shoe or prepare afterschool snacks. What if you could find a villa in Italy and stay a whole month? Of course the villa would come with a cook and maid so your relaxing hours would not be interrupted by such mundane chores as preparing meals and cleaning up!

The responsibilities women have within their families, at work, and church demand dedication, persistence, and the fortitude just to survive. When my three children were still at home, if you had talked to me about the influence I had on others, I might have laughed out loud. I was just trying to get through the week! Influence is a topic, however, that actually is very important for every woman, regardless of her age or life stage. When we are parenting, we want to influence our children to grow "in the nurture and admonition of the Lord" (Ephesians 6:4). When they are teens, we try to influence them in making godly decisions that will shape their adult lives. We watch from a distance as they go off to college, choose careers, and select mates. We pray that our past influence is strong enough to guide them to seek God's face.

But what happens if—or, perhaps, *when*—we don't believe we really have any influence? If our self-esteem isn't healthy, our decisions and interactions with other people will not reflect our real worth and potential influence. We all have influence. The question is, of course, what kind? This chapter is about how important it is for every woman to have a mentor. A mentoring relationship is one of the most critical relationships we can have and one that will maximize our influence. Read the following account of another found object, and then we'll talk some more about the benefits of mentoring, what to look for in a mentor, and what we, in turn, can do for others.

Several years ago my husband and I participated in a missions event on Hawaii's Big Island. Our activities focused on the city of Hilo located on the eastern side of Hawaii. There was a big luau to kick off the event, and we fellowshipped together as we got ready for the various projects. Everything was to culminate on July 4 when families went to the park at the water's edge to watch fireworks and have picnics.

During the week we helped paint a small church and spruce up the grounds. My husband worked on cutting back the vines that were threatening to take over the building, and I painted parking barriers. We ate lunch in the shade of a huge tree on the edge of the church property. Others installed sprinklers at a church/preschool center. I was asked to share my testimony with children and youth during Sunday Bible study on the north end of the island. We had good experiences and enjoyed our time in God's paradise.

After the week of missions activity, my husband and I stayed for a brief vacation in a rented condo that was right on the ocean. Ah! The surf pounding all day and night was wonderful. I was taking an online graduate course at the time, so I worked on that in the

In a sea of black, crusted lava something was growing; something was changing the wasteland

mornings, and then we took tourist excursions in the afternoon. Of course, each one included spending time at one of Hawaii's famous beaches. We took a rutted dirt road as far as we could and then got out and walked a short distance.

I was snapping photos and panning the devastation caused in 1982 by the hot, flowing lava. I saw something. Something caught my attention. I moved my camera back to take another look and discovered a sight that was seemingly impossible. There, peeking up from the hard, black lava was a small, green plant! It was only about three inches tall, so it's a wonder I saw it at all. In a sea of black, crusted lava something was growing; something was changing the wasteland caused by the volcanic eruption all those years ago.

I suddenly became a photographer on a mission! Captured for our vacation album, I will never forget the beauty of that plant rising up out of what we thought was a place where nothing productive or beautiful could exist again. God had manifested Himself in this example of simple beauty, memorializing His faithfulness to bring healing and mercy to anyone trusting in Him. Isn't our salvation experience just like that? We are surrounded by darkness and life's hard experiences, but when we trust in Him, God will bring forth new life in us—life through His Son Jesus—and we will be set on a path toward many new beginnings.

But this story isn't over! After I was satisfied with the photographs, we got back in the car and retraced our drive down the dirt road and found a small park right on the beach. We were in Hawaii, after all! My husband chose to sit in the shade to read. I took my beach towel and low folding beach chair out to the sand and set everything up to make myself comfortable. The sun was warm, the surf was loud, and life was good! I had been there for about 30 minutes when a youngish man and woman came down to the shore shelf and prepared to enjoy the sun's warmth too. I got the distinct impression that they had not seen each other in a long time.

Because they were sitting so close to me, I could overhear their conversation. I didn't eavesdrop intentionally, but once I heard what the man was saying I was riveted. He began to share about a time when he felt God moving in his life. He told about his life before Christ and the difficulties he had experienced. He related that when he became a believer, everything seemed different and new. He had moved from darkness to light. He commented that he knew he needed to grow and learn about God so he began searching for someone to help him do that. He admitted to his companion that he never found anyone to "take him under his wing." He visited various churches but found no fellowship, no one who took an interest in him personally.

Here was a young seedling seeking sustenance with no success. He had found Christ in spite of the hardness of his life (lava?) and was trying to grow as he sensed he should. I sat in stunned silence as he voiced his reflections about his early Christian life. Sadly, his story ended there with the admission that he had never truly found anyone to help and guide him. What a waste! It certainly is not God's intention that His new plants be left to fend for themselves, futilely looking for fellowship and help in growing spiritually. He has given that responsibility to believers.

Two young plants trying to survive—both in a rock-solid bed of lava. Growth seemed impossible. I couldn't help but think that the plant in the lava bed might have a better chance of continued growth than the young man. There is a word for the type of guidance the young man had sought: *mentoring*. He needed (and deserved) a pastor, a believing co-worker, or a small Bible study group to provide him with the tools to grow in Christ.

Do you think it was an accident that I overheard the conversation at the beach right after I'd seen that plant surviving in the lava bed? I don't think so. When things like that happen to me, I sit up, take notice, and try to take in what God is telling me. I have thought about that day on the beach many times, and I am convinced that one thing I can do is to encourage women to find someone to mentor them. You may have done enough reading to realize that mentors fall into many different categories. Sometimes we need a mentor to guide us in our vocation or profession. Other times we need someone who will help us grow spiritually. A mentor can be anyone who is willing to invest time and energy into helping another to develop a realistic view of their abilities, talents, roles, social traits, beliefs, and intellectual capacity.

If you've never had another woman mentor you, it's time! There's one word of caution that I would give you at this point:

women should only be mentored by women. Now, I know that it's often difficult for women to find professional mentors because there aren't as many successful women in many professions as there are men. However, many traps arise if the mentoring relationship isn't woman to woman. You understand what I'm saying and why, right? Good. So, let's look at the benefits of mentoring.

You may be thinking, *She's saying all of this, but what's in it for me?* Here's a short list of benefits. I'm sure you'll think of others as you read.

1. A mentor can give you insights from her own experiences that will help you look at things you need to change . . . and maybe some things you can't change.

2. A mentor can challenge you to stretch yourself and motivate you to make the changes she's helped you discover you need to make.

   I read a humorous story about a man who tried to enter his mule in the famous Kentucky Derby. He was told in no uncertain terms that he couldn't do that and that his mule had no chance of winning the race. He replied, "Oh, I know that. I just thought the association would do him good." (Illustration from John Maxwell's book *Leadership Gold.*) When we associate with women who have more experience than we do in a certain area, some of it is bound to rub off on us!

3. A mentor can help you develop a plan especially for you and your personal growth. (Remember, this growth can be spiritual, professional, social, or any number of other areas.)

John Maxwell cites an Asian Tar-Tar tribal curse they used on their enemies: "May you stay in one place . . . forever!" How disastrous that would be for any of us! And yet, isn't that exactly what we do? Because we lack the confidence to move forward, we tread water, or walk in place.

4. A mentor can teach you to look at your experiences and evaluate them in order to learn from them.

A mentor can teach you how to make sound decisions. I have heard someone call this a "filter." When parents make decisions about raising their children, they are using an established filter. When you think through ethical situations that might arise at work, you are using your moral filter to help you ahead of time.

I hope you are beginning to realize that you need a mentor! There is a lot of information out there about how to be a good mentor but not as much has been written about finding one. As you've been reading, you may have thought of a woman who would be perfect to help you develop a spiritual growth plan. There may be someone at work who has the ability to encourage you in your profession. Your aunt or grandmother may be just the person to guide you in increasing your influence in your family relationships.

But, what if you have just relocated and don't know many people? Maybe your family all lives in another state? You just recently joined a new church, so who would you ask? And, anyway, what would you ask her or expect from her? Here are a few characteristics you should consider as you start looking for a woman to guide, encourage, and teach you.

Search for a mentor who will be honest with you.

- shows you how to behave, speak, interact with others by her actions, speech, relationships.
- commits to helping you. (Read 1 Timothy 5:2.)
- shares her failures as well as her successes with you.
- can teach. Not everyone is a teacher! Look for someone who can verbalize how she has done things so you can learn from her.
- believes in you and in your abilities. She needs to see your potential.
- will help you chart progress toward a healthier self-esteem and put your dreams into action.
- is successful in her own right. Her reputation precedes her.

One last thing you need to look for in a mentor: someone who will follow your agenda, not something she wants to do. Bobb Biehl has written an excellent book on mentoring, *Mentoring: Confidence in Finding a Mentor and Becoming One,* and he says, "What you're really looking for is a person that you know cares for you, believes in you, and encourages you."

If you are serious about finding a mentor, you need to ask yourself some interview-type questions. I know, forming questions require thinking and sometimes that's more energy than you have, right? Stop a minute and read through my suggestions. Don't stress over all the implications, just read the questions and be quiet for a minute or two. Let God speak to you about one or more of them. He will reveal the direction you need to take as you begin your search for a mentor and healthier self-esteem.

- How are you investing in yourself?
- Are you living and working in your strengths?

- How open are you to taking advice?
- Are you willing to change?
- What if the change isn't your idea?
- Are you teachable?
- Can you take negative feedback?
- What do your relationships look like?
- Can you own up to your mistakes?
- Do you ever evaluate your experiences?
- Who is in your sphere of influence?
- What do you want a mentor to do for you?

You've read about it. You've thought about it. Now what? It's time to take action. Begin now to look for a woman who can be a mentor to you!

As I look back on my own life, I realize I have had several strong mentors. I was fortunate to have a supervisor in my early work years who took an interest in me beyond the assignments she gave me. Frances, the friend I mentioned in the introduction, not only apprenticed me in library science but also she established a relationship with me that lasted after our working relationship ended. She taught me skills I needed to be a good children's librarian, and at the same time she was modeling for me a passion for reading that has stayed with me through married life, motherhood, career choices, and even beyond her death. The lessons she modeled for me and the professional attitude she demonstrated made a remarkable difference in my life.

Cate was a spiritual mentor for me. I did not meet Cate until she became the Bible study leader for our young women's missions group. She had been retired longer than I'd been alive! What an example of spiritual stability she gave us. Her commitment to studying God's Word was unparalleled. Her passion for ministry showed us that we each needed to participate in reaching out to others in Christ's name. Her faithfulness in giving to missions from her limited income said more than she ever could have verbalized. Cate mentored an entire group at one time! We met at her house because she didn't drive. Her failing eyesight and other limitations never dictated her involvement in missions or her commitment to God's work.

My mother was a pastor's wife for almost 71 years. Her involvement in missions was of such long standing that it was simply part of her identity. As a child, I learned to use scissors by helping her make invitations to women's missions meetings. I learned how to lead workshops by watching her. I learned how to make detailed event plans by seeing her in action. Her passion for missions ran ahead of her paving the way for her creativity and ability to involve others. She encouraged me to step outside my comfort zone and use my own brand of creativity.

In an earlier chapter, I talked about Ethel and how she patiently led me through the frustrations and demands of a denominational leadership position. She still serves as a sounding board, even though she is now retired.

Evelyn was the girls' teacher everyone wanted! While her influence on me was brief, it had an impact on me in several ways. Girls could hardly wait to be nine years old because that meant we would move up to her class. Her class, you see, not only had cushions on the folding chairs, she had the books of the Bible on wooden blocks to help us recite them in order. You knew, when you were in her class, that you were special!

These women helped me begin my journey toward a healthy self-esteem.

Can you handle one more question? Once you're a mentee (the one being mentored), are you always a mentee?

Are we to develop a "sit and soak" mentality? Absolutely not! As we learn from other women, we should be willing to become mentors ourselves. Mentoring another woman doesn't mean we can't still have our own mentors. Far from it. We need to stay fresh so we should continue those mentoring relationships for as long as we need them. I have learned a lot from the mentors in my life, and I believe very strongly that we should give back, however, when we can.

In the past several years, God has given me opportunities to establish five very rewarding mentoring relationships. I mentored two women doing graduate work: one in person, the other long-distance via Skype and email. Those were formal relationships complete with contractual agreements. I mentored a friend for several years to take a major leadership role in a large women's organization. She now says, "That's why you suggested I do that! Now I understand!" There is nothing more satisfying than seeing how God works in women's lives for His glory.

I was approached by a mother of three young boys to mentor her in missions leadership. She wanted direction in planning and executing strategies for adult involvement in local ministries. Because she did not have child care readily available, we met every Monday morning via email. We both had a good time and learned from each other. (You do realize—don't you—that a mentor learns from her mentee?) Through our pastor, another woman asked to meet with me to talk about being a spiritual mentor for her. We met every week and discussed how God wants us to grow in His Word, listen to His prompting, and be open to follow His leading.

So, here's the bottom line: There's no doubt that when we learn, change, and improve, our self-esteems will be healthier! Our influence will increase and grow stronger. As mentors, we will probably never know how far-reaching our influence is. Biehl said it well in *Mentoring: Confidence in Finding a Mentor and Becoming One*, "It may be the way you change history. It may be the way you make a major difference. It may be the reason you are on this earth today, to mentor even one person who wouldn't make it without you."

Found Treasure

AND A LITTLE CHILD
SHALL LEAD THEM

I HAVE A FRIEND WHO, IN A FORMER LIFE, WAS A NURSE. While she isn't active in that profession any longer, her compassion and concern for others has found another outlet—she teaches CPR (cardiopulmonary resuscitation) in local high schools at the invitation of the administration. Now, this CPR is not the medical kind of CPR. She and several other women developed a curriculum to teach teens how to make good decisions about their relationships. "Creating Positive Relationships" is a way to introduce students to godly principles about relationships that we have. It is not openly taught as a religious approach to relationships, but when the opportunity arises, my friend and the other teachers walk through the open door!

We all have relationships in our lives that are healthy. All of us have relationships that are not good for our self-esteem too. Even though a relationship is not currently in your life or mine doesn't mean it isn't still affecting us. Broken relationships with our parents, issues with our brothers and sisters, conflicts with friends (or former friends!), and harmful relationships in the workplace still impact how we relate to people. In other words, the co-worker who undermined us at work five years ago influences the relationships we have today at work. Dysfunctional family relationships in childhood orchestrate the ones we establish with our own children. The courtship that led to our marriage is shaped by the marriage relationship our parents had, or didn't have.

Let's face it—we can't get away from the relationships in our lives! I found a description of relationships in *Words to Live by for Women* that states clearly how important relationships are in our lives. "Relationships define family and community. Relationships spawn churches, cities, and nations. Relationships provide motivation for fighting evil and doing good and learning love because you know these people well enough to care what happens to them."

When our relationships are positive, our self-esteem can be healthy too. On the negative side, however, we know that when our relationships are poisonous, every area of our lives is affected. It's the old story of everyone being upset and the dog is the one that bears the brunt of their frustrations! What determines how successful we are relating to others? Is there some recipe for having healthy relationships? How can we avoid making decisions that put us in relationships that are unhealthy for us and our self-esteem?

The Harvard School of Public Health's studies on relationships concluded that our social networks help us live longer. Researchers found healthy relationships are more accurate in predicting health and a long life than gender, race, age, or even poor health habits such as smoking (Donna Carter, *10 Smart Things Women Can Do*). Does it make sense, then, that unhealthy relationships can make us ill? And that they can cause our self-esteem to suffer?

While there is no formula that's guaranteed to give us healthy relationships and foster healthy self-esteem, there are three things that directly affect our ability to establish and maintain strong, healthy interactions with people in our lives. As you read the following discussions, stop and think about the relationships in your life. Are there things you can do to work toward better connections with others?

First, *your past* plays a tremendous role in your perception of yourself. Your family (its makeup, your birth order, the roles your mother and father played, ethnic background) never stops influencing how you feel about yourself and your accomplishments. Where does the influence of your family stop and your personhood begin? This is a difficult question to answer. There isn't a day that I don't think about something that happened when I was a child. A smell triggers vacation memories. Spaghetti reminds me of the time my father made me eat all of my food (I was a terrible eater in those days)! To this day I can't stand spaghetti. Even a photograph reminds me of that night in the kitchen when that cold Italian pasta and sauce and green beans congealed on my plate. You have memories that surface every day, too, don't you? Some memories bring smiles to our faces while others make us grit our teeth and we think, *I'll never do that!* (Note: An exercise in appendix B on p. 179 focuses on how your past influences you and your behavior.)

Second, *expectations* dictate much of how we behave. You may say you've moved past all that, that you don't pay any attention to what others expect you to do, but you and I know that isn't true! Are others' expectations always realistic? Of course not. If our own expectations aren't grounded in reality, why would we think others have a better view? How much you let these expectations dominate your life will be seen in your self-esteem. Every woman must set boundaries in her relationships. If she doesn't, she will spend her days trying to be everything to everyone. Just the other day I received a catalog in the mail advertising all kinds of gifts especially for women. Under "sassy" T-shirts was one that read, *I am who I am . . . Your approval isn't needed.* When a woman is secure in her boundaries, she will not feel the need to prove herself over and over.

Mahatma Gandhi, talking about self-esteem said, "They cannot take away our self respect if we do not give it to them." Is this true? I think it is. If we can cope with others' expectations, keep our own expectations in line, and learn to handle criticism and even rejection, then we will move toward a healthy self-esteem.

Third, *acceptance* plays a tremendous role in how we view ourselves. Part of being accepted is the tendency to be a people pleaser. We as women expend a lot of energy getting others to accept us. *Runaway Bride*, a 1999 chick flick starring Julia Roberts, is a great example of the lengths to which we'll go to be accepted. If you've seen the movie, do you remember how Julia's character tried to change to become the kind of woman her love interest at the time wanted? When Richard Gere's character entered her life, he accused her of not even knowing how she liked her eggs! Later scenes show her preparing scrambled eggs, poached eggs, and fried eggs. She realized he was right, and she needed to figure out what *she* really liked. It was a funny movie, but I wonder how many of us do the same things Julia's character did!

Look at the story about Jesus and the Samaritan woman (John 4:1–26). Meeting her at the local watering spot, Jesus engaged her in conversation. As we read the story, it is easy to see that this woman's relationships have been less than healthy, and her decisions have painted her into a corner. She is not only despised because of her race, but her choices have ostracized her. She learned that day in the noonday heat that there was only one person's acceptance she needed to have—God's.

Here's the issue of having healthy relationships in a nutshell: there are only two relationships we can count on. First, your relationship to God through His Son Jesus is the ultimate affirming relationship. Second, to a lesser degree, you can count on the relationships you have with people who you are determined to love no matter what. According to *Words to Live by for Women*, "Relationships are a test of your Christian commitment and your greatest challenge."

As your self-esteem grows, you will be faced with opportunities to relate to others in new ways. You may choose to teach a Bible study for women or lead a children's singing group. You may volunteer to be a reading tutor at the neighborhood elementary school or help with a community fund-raiser or county political campaign. Positive relationships will help you set your past aside, rise above others' expectations, and establish new relationships with the world around you.

Before I began working with adult women, I worked with children in various capacities. I was active in my boys' elementary school parent/teacher association and coordinated the annual Santa's Workshop which provided 3,000 gifts under $1 for children to purchase for their families at Christmas. I have led a children's choir, directed a large preschool ministry, and worked in Vacation Bible Schools in four states. The following found object story relates how I believe God uses us and our relationships to touch others' lives.

I have had a longtime love for old furniture. I went through an oak phase, and everything I bought reflected a period of time when oak was highly regarded. I eventually branched out into other woods, so today you can walk through my home and see walnut chifforobes and dressers, oak china cabinets, and

When I opened one of the drawers, I found an unexpected treasure!

even handmade pine items. There are stories connected to almost every one of them. If I had space, I'd tell you about how to get large, cumbersome mirrors and cabinets home in a station wagon!

I've attended many estate sales, but one of the most rewarding ones resulted in my purchasing a beautiful golden oak dresser with a mirror. The piece was just the right size for my daughter's room. I checked out the dresser carefully to make sure there were no broken drawers or wobbly legs. When I opened one of the drawers, I found an unexpected treasure! Stuffed in the back of one drawer were two long baby dresses.

The dresses were beautiful though they were dingy with age. The gowns were made from thin, white lawn fabric and were embellished by cutwork embroidery. Someone had lovingly sewn the garments, and I longed for them to be mine. I approached the estate salesperson and told her what I had found. "Anything you find in the drawers is yours." I could hardly wait to load up my new treasure and take it home.

It was easy to see that the child's clothing was not particularly valuable. Obviously, they held no significant place in family memories, but they were treasures to me. While I could easily have paid for them separately, having found them stored away in the back of a drawer made them special. These found objects started my vintage clothing collection. I added aprons, linens, and small clothing pieces until I had a cedar chest full. An entire collection evolved because of these two found objects that had once belonged to some sweet, innocent child. Thinking about little children automatically leads my thoughts to experiences I have had as a teacher in various capacities.

Some of my most meaningful experiences have been teaching children about missions. I began my teaching journey as a young married woman. The church I attended did not have any leaders for the preschool missions group. When I realized my own children wouldn't have a missions teacher, I made the commitment to teach them about missions and how God loved the world. I quickly discovered they were eager learners, and what I taught them went home with them to their parents. In essence, I was teaching them too.

My small group of little girls and boys began to grow, and I enlisted and trained a young single woman to help me. Two special incidents remain in my mind even after all of these years. We were learning about missionaries in Japan, and I heard about a Japanese deer park with a petting zoo not far from where we lived—a perfect outing for the group. I enlisted several parents to go with us, and we set off with sack lunches on the church bus to learn about Japan. (Can you believe I actually took 12 preschoolers on a bus trip?) The adventure was so special that a little girl who broke her arm the day before the trip refused to miss the adventure, so her mother came with us, cushioning her arm on a pillow. Years later the girl's mother told me that her daughter talked about the trip for years.

Another special experience happened near Christmas. Our preschoolers were learning about missions work in Mexico. As the time for a special Christmas missions offering approached, I decided preschoolers could learn about giving. I had a yucca pod "tree" and made little paper sombreros as ornaments. The children were encouraged to bring five cents each week and we put a sombrero on the tree for every nickel given. Soon the entire tree was covered with sombreros! The children were learning that their gifts would help tell people all over the world about Jesus.

The years I taught preschoolers about God's love for the world and how they could tell their families and friends about Jesus were very rewarding ones. As anyone who works with preschoolers can tell you, there is rarely a dull minute with them! My grandchildren—just like some of your young children and grandchildren, no doubt—provide us with some profound and hilarious statements we will remember long after they've forgotten.

Not long ago my daughter's family went out to eat. Her youngest son, Ian, ordered root beer to drink with his meal, and it came in a bottle along with a frosted mug. When his dad asked him how much he wanted poured into the mug, he thought a second and then replied, "Fill me up to Jesus!" Where that came from or what his thought process was at the time we don't know, but his statement is a good one illustrating how we should approach our daily walk with God's Son. We, too, should desire to be filled up with Jesus. Being filled with Jesus may send us in directions we might not have chosen or even thought of. Ian's statement, while extremely humorous at the time, reminds us that we need to be aware of our influence.

Years ago my father and mother were traveling to New Zealand to participate in a preaching crusade. An offering appeal was made during a Sunday morning worship service, and what happened after that service motivated him to write a brief account, which he submitted to our national mission-sending agency. The story shows how everyone, regardless of their age, can participate in proclaiming the good news of Jesus. My father was a strong advocate of mission support and involvement throughout almost 60 years of pastoral ministry. He rejoices today at the feet of Jesus for the privilege of preaching the wonderful stories of God's faithfulness and love.

In an article entitled "Two Pennies Worth of Love," my father tells the story of a preschooler's love:

> She had waited for the crowd to leave the church foyer and for those who had a personal word for the pastor to finish their talking. It was only then that the shy four-year-old approached the pastor, looking up, holding high an outstretched hand. There in a little girl's hand were two pennies.
>
> An appeal had been made for the church members to have a part in sending the pastor on an overseas preaching mission. The mother explained that

the little girl wanted to give her two pennies, all the money she had, to help in this mission. In the earnest simplicity of a child, she gave all that she had. It was just a two-penny gift, but it was a gift of love. Two pennies worth of love doesn't sound like much love until you know that it represented all that a small child had to give. When sincere love is present, the size of the gifts is immaterial. . . .

Whether it be the exceedingly small gift of one who is in need himself, or the larger gift of one who gives far more than he can afford, or the lavish offering of one who is wealthy, or the two pennies held out in the grimy hand of a little child, it is love that makes that offering "a sweet smelling sacrifice" acceptable unto our Lord.

"And a little child will lead them" (Isaiah 11:6 NIV).

What if my self-esteem had not grown to the point where I established relationships with those preschoolers and children? Who would have influenced them? Would someone else have stepped in to take the responsibility? Maybe. Maybe not.

Let's review: Our relationships are often dictated by our past relationships, positive or dysfunctional. Relationships with our world may be limited or ineffective because we let others' expectations and criticisms dominate our actions rather than focusing on how God has created us to relate to Him and others. How we relate to the world impacts our immediate lives, but it also makes an eternal difference to others. "So whether we are in the body or away from this body, our goal is to please him" (2 Corinthians 5:9 NLT).

AUTOBIOGRAPHY IN FIVE SHORT CHAPTERS

I.

I walk down the street. There is a deep hole in the sidewalk. I fall in. I am lost . . . I am helpless. It isn't my fault. It takes forever to find a way out.

II.

I walk down the same street. There is a deep hole in the sidewalk. I pretend I don't see it. I fall in again. I can't believe I am in the same place, but it isn't my fault. It still takes a long time to get out.

III.

I walk down the same street. There is a deep hole in the sidewalk. I see it there. I still fall in . . . it's a habit. My eyes are open. I know where I am. It is my fault. I get out immediately.

IV.

I walk down the same street. There is a deep hole in the sidewalk. I walk around it.

V.

I walk down another street.

Portia Nelson, *There's a Hole in My Sidewalk* (Hillsboro, OR: Beyond Words Publishing, 1993), xi–xii.

Found Treasure

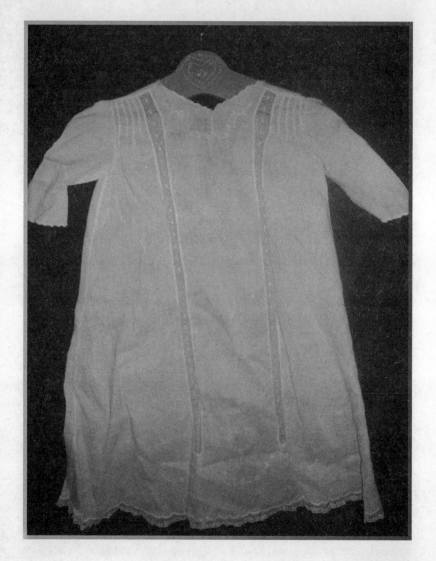

GONE BUT NOT FORGOTTEN

FOR FIVE OR SIX YEARS I SAW CABLE NETWORK television programs and read articles about an interesting event in *Country Living* magazine. The World's Longest Yard Sale. Every year I would sigh deeply and remark, "I wish I could do that someday." That someday came this past summer! Relocating to the Midwest, I found myself only about two hours away from "the route." I began making plans early in the year to participate and enlisted my daughter to make the trip with me. We began making a list of items we would need: our van, blankets, bungee cords, and rope. Could we tie things on top of the van? We would probably need a cooler, and of course we would wear tennis shoes and comfortable clothing.

What in the world were we getting ready to do? No, we weren't trying out for the *Survivor* television program. We weren't making plans to dismantle a building (but of course, that could happen!). This yard sale is a continuous string of sales that begins in Michigan and follows Route 127 as far as Gadsden, Alabama. We joined the route in Kentucky and had time to drive as far as south as Chattanooga, Tennessee. What a great experience! We set some ground rules as we began driving—we would not follow signs that led us off the main route. While "Barn Sale" might be enticing, it also might be off the route five miles, and we didn't have that much time.

The first half day out on the "trail" had to be one of the hottest days of the summer. It was August, after all. We almost melted into our shoes as we trudged over plowed fields to the tents, canopies, and tables that were loaded with hard-to-find, must-buy items. We looked until rain threatened and the sky got dark. The next day was cooler, and we got an early start. We parked on the highway, in parking lots, on church properties, and even in tree groves in our search for bargains and unusual things we *had* to have. We each had a mental list of things we wanted so our search was smart, specific, and spirited. That day we drove, parked, and hunted for 12 hours! We felt the best deal was just down the road, on that back table.

I knew that this trip was not going to result in a lot of found objects. These things were for sale, disqualifying them from the strictest found objects category. We found a huge equine showing arena, which promised countless treasures under its roof. With approximately 75 separate displays, interesting things filled bins, tables, and leaned against the walls. When I entered the arena, I immediately spied an old water pump. A water pump was on my list for my new backyard! I was like a homing pigeon as I took off toward it. After talking to the old farmer who had brought it to sell, I discovered that it came from a farm in my own state. *Perfect*, I thought. The price wasn't perfect, though. However, after some creative negotiating, the unusual water pump and its bucket belonged to me!

As my daughter and I continued to walk up and down the aisles of the giant structure, we found one booth run by a woman whose interest ran toward household items. Almost everything in the booth related to a woman's life. Fascinated, I began to look carefully at what she had displayed in boxes, crates, and baskets. A small cardboard box caught my attention. It was filled with small black-and-white photographs. They were evidently snaps taken of school-age children, most likely actual school pictures.

The children were about fourth through sixth grade, and their clothing indicated they were not from affluent families. Their clothes ran from print dresses to overalls, similar to photos I've seen from the 1940s. My guess is they were from a rural area, perhaps a farming community. I was drawn to the one boy because of a photo I had seen in one of my mother-in-law's family photo albums, a snapshot of my husband at age 10 or 12 years old, a scrawny youngster, the smallest of his brothers and sisters. His hair was unruly, and honestly, he looked as if he'd been thrown away!

I stood in the booth for a long time wondering how I would ever use the photos. I didn't know the children's names or anything about them. I certainly reacted to their evident lack of material possessions. I finally decided that I couldn't justify buying them. I'm sure you have heard about buyer's remorse. Well buyer's remorse also can work in the reverse—when you see something you really want, but don't purchase it, you later regret not doing so. That's the kind of remorse I've had since August. I regret that I didn't choose several to bring home. Why is the question that still bothers me, but I believe I have a partial answer.

The photos reminded me of an incident that my husband told me about during our courtship. His family was a poor one.

Both his mother and father worked several jobs trying to make ends meet and to feed their large family. He learned to bake and cook because he was too young to go to work but too old to do nothing. He became the family cookie, pie, and cake baker. (This has been a great blessing to me in our

My husband's photograph could easily have been in that shoebox last August.

marriage!) During the early 1940s, his family moved onto a World War II munitions depot outside a small Nebraska town, where his parents found jobs. We recently drove out to the depot (still there, but permanently closed) and took pictures of the concrete block structure that housed their entire family. We also drove by the two-story brick building where he and his brother and sisters attended school. It had a desolate air about it as it stood abandoned, encased by a chain-link fence. Going back into town was a trip back in time that brought back very few pleasant memories for my husband.

There was one bright spot in my husband's life at this time, however—something happened that changed his life forever. One night he heard the sound of music coming from outside the apartment where the family lived. Curious, he left the house and followed the sounds. There under a dim streetlight was a small group of people singing hymns. Once a crowd gathered, someone shared the simple message of Jesus and how He could transform lives when persons trusted Him. That night under the streetlight, Jan made his decision to follow Christ. He was 12 years old, too young to drive in to church, too young to be an active church member. But his decision was a real one. Through the years, he has never wavered from the belief that what he experienced gave him new purpose and direction in life.

We couldn't find the church in town that he had attended sporadically because, after all, more than 60 years have gone by! While the memory of those years in poverty has faded a bit, the new life in Jesus has not. This is actually just part one of the story, though.

Several years ago I was asked to be the guest speaker for a large women's retreat. Women from two states attended the event— Kansas and Nebraska. Knowing that some of the women were Nebraskans, I intentionally included Jan's childhood story in one of my speeches that weekend since we were meeting in Kansas. I used it to illustrate how a small group of people made an eternal difference in a young boy's life. After the worship session, a woman made a beeline to talk to me. She was so excited. She and her husband had been part of the group that went out to the munitions depot on a regular basis. It is likely that they were there the night Jan made his decision for Christ!

Now I realize that for you, the reader, it might be difficult to see how my mind jumped from a yard-sale school photographs from the past to a salvation experience, but that's exactly what happened. My husband's photograph could easily have been in that shoebox last August. His photograph would have shown that he, too, didn't have the best of clothes. It could have shown that touch of despair we often see in photographs taken of poverty-stricken people. If those committed Christians had not gone out to the depot that one night, that look of hopelessness might have been reflected in his eyes for many years, perhaps forever.

We don't always know about the results of our ministry and witnessing. Scripture tells us we aren't responsible for the results. Our obligation is to obey God's commandments to make disciples. All too often we mistakenly think our efforts have to be grandiose when, actually, the opposite is true. When we share Christ in word or by our behavior and attitude, our witness will not return to us empty. "So is my word that goes out from my mouth: It will not return to me empty, but will accomplish what I desire and achieve the purpose for which I sent it" (Isaiah 55:11 NIV). We are accountable for the sharing; God honors our obedience.

Because one small church was faithful to reach out to those who normally would have fallen outside their influence, at least one person will spend eternity in heaven. Jan was baptized and became active in a church in Southern California, where his family later moved. He attended a Christian college and has been active in a church since that time. His commitment to the local church has led him to serve as a deacon, lead Bible studies, direct Sunday School, disciple new believers, and serve on various committees. His commitment to missions took him to El Salvador where he was the logistics coordinator for missions teams. By the time God called him to do that, he had lost almost all of his hearing, but he answered the call anyway. He says, "If a deaf, dizzy man can go on a missions trip, anyone can!"

I regret that I didn't at least inquire about the cost of the school snapshots that day on my yard-sale trip. They wouldn't have been terribly expensive and would be a tangible reminder of a child's life long ago. The miniature photographs would remind me to be faithful in all God asks me to do, even in the small things. I didn't buy a photo, but I can easily remember the look of deprivation on the faces of the children. May I never forget my obligation to be faithful and that the results of my faithfulness will be eternal.

We can succumb to life's circumstances and fail to look around to see the needs of other women. We can become negligent in sharing Christ with others. Can this tendency be remotely connected to self-esteem? Have you ever felt the Holy Spirit nudging you to speak to someone only to retreat into yourself, saying nothing? Is that a self-esteem issue or simply a lack of caring?

One of my favorite passages is 2 Corinthians 8:10 in *The Message*: "Do what you can, not what you can't. The heart regulates the hand." There are some weeks when I stop and think about how I have reached out to others in Jesus' name and realize my hand has been empty all week! What does that say about my heart? Am I uninterested or insecure?

How does our self-esteem affect how we relate to others? I'm not talking about our established life relationships here (marriage, family, etc.), but how does our self-esteem help or hinder our efforts to tell people what Jesus means to us personally? If we feel unprepared, there are steps we can take to feel more confident in talking to others about God's Son. If we are still extremely uneasy about giving witness as a Christ follower, perhaps our perception of ourselves is standing in the way.

What is God's answer to self-esteem? Matthew 10:39 (NIV) gives us an answer about how we are to regard ourselves, "Whoever finds their life will lose it, and whoever loses their life for my sake will find it." We are not to focus on ourselves but to love and serve God and others. Setting our self-esteem "flaws" aside will help us realize that no amount of achievement will produce a real feeling of security and love. That comes only as we relate to God as our heavenly Father.

Paul speaks to this idea in Galatians 2:20 (NKJV), "I have been crucified with Christ; it is no longer I who live, but Christ lives in me." I don't know about you, but this verse is tremendously liberating to me! I don't have to worry that my words aren't eloquent enough or that my walk with the Lord has been a stumbling one. As I allow Christ to live through me, I am able to present Him in such a way that others are drawn to Him. This doesn't mean I suddenly become proficient and polished in my telling others about what Christ means to me. Acknowledging that Christ lives in me gives me a focus outside myself, a focus that translates into stepping around my self-esteem a bit in order to bring the good news to those around me.

Kay Strom, in *Perfect in His Eyes* said, "God loves you. And he wants you to love yourself. But he also wants you to move beyond that self-love." Do you agree with her statement? Can we let our unhealthy self-esteem keep us from doing what we should be doing as believers? *But*, you say, this is risky business! You are exactly right! Serving others means getting to know people as people. It means learning their names, about their families, in other words, going beneath the surface. When we decide to share Christ, we cannot hold people at arm's length.

I recently met a woman who volunteered to work with women from other parts of the world who have moved to her city. The ministry center she works through opened not long ago and already ministers to more than 60 ethnic groups in the neighborhood surrounding the center! This woman helps immigrant women with limited English skills find a way to earn money to help their struggling families. While their husbands are working low-paying jobs, the women are becoming fledgling artisans. Making soap, jewelry, and textile pieces, they supplement their families' incomes while learning about God at the same time. Risky? Yes! Time-consuming? Definitely! Challenging? You bet!

A popular music group, Casting Crowns, came to a large city near us, and my daughter and I bought tickets to attend. We were up in the "crow's nest" but still had a decent view of the stage several miles away. It had been a long time since I'd been to a live concert—do you know everyone stands the entire time during a concert now? Oh my! Well, at any rate, I thoroughly enjoyed the music that evening. I especially enjoyed having their words up on the screen! One song particularly touched me, "Between the Altar and the Door." Find a CD or download this song, and I think you'll agree that its lyrics are powerful. The thought behind the song is that we are moved to serve during a worship experience, and we tell God we are willing to do what He wants us to do. But, something happens. Between the altar and the door we change our minds, the world floods in, and our insecurities take over. Our self-esteem tells us we aren't capable of sharing properly. It convinces us we really don't have much of a testimony. It assures us that someone else who is stronger in the Lord will take our place.

Snapshots and photo albums offer memories and insights. In the middle of my reminiscing, God has impressed me again that I am accountable to tell others about Him. Maybe you are like me—I have a tendency to think what I share has to be of *Star Wars* magnitude. You know, full sound effects and technical *hoopla* (another word for grand displays).

God calls me (and you, my friend) to give testimony of Him in small ways: an encouraging word, preparing a meal, crocheting an afghan, sharing your life in Christ. You know, like a small group of Christ followers singing praises to God under a street light!

An added note: This past summer I made another road trip to find bargains at the World's Longest Yard Sale, I finally found the equestrian center where I'd seen the school snapshots. This time I was going to buy some! But the vendor wasn't there this year. Missing another opportunity to buy a bit of history that had come to mean something spiritual to me was like most second chances. When I miss an opportunity—buying, sharing, encouraging— I almost never get a second chance. As the old blacksmithing proverb says, "Strike while the iron is hot."

Found Treasure

CHAPTER 8

JUST A BOY?

THIS CHAPTER IS GOING TO FOCUS ON MINISTRY. NOW, in your mind you just reacted in one of several ways: You said to yourself, *not another motivational talk!* Or, you may have thought, *I've done ministry in the past, and I'm over it!* It could be that one or two of you shuddered because of a bad experience you've had in the past when you tried to do something for someone else. Perhaps, the topic brought pleasant memories of rewarding experiences where God blessed you with stamina, insight, and creativity.

How a woman responds to ministry may reflect her self-esteem. Have you ever thought of it in that way? We have a tendency (or is it an ability?) to dissect issues for motivation, hidden nuances, and meaning until the men in our lives shout, "Enough! You've beaten this to death!" But, it's what a lot of us do. So, when it comes to becoming involved in ministry, we might approach it in the same way. However, just because we dissect something doesn't mean we will come to the right answer!

Ministry is a very personal thing, as it should be. As Christ followers we are called to minister to others. As we dissect ministry, we need to be honest about why we shy away from it. Could it be that you don't believe you are capable of relating to others in this way? Do you have heart palpitations just thinking about going into an unknown situation where you might be called upon to be flexible and take a risk to share? These are difficult questions, aren't they? Let's look at God's Word to see what He says about extending ourselves in ministry. The rest of this chapter will be a series of questions ending with my found treasure story, which I hope will illustrate how every one of us is to find her ministry niche.

What is God's answer to our self-esteem issues?

Look up Matthew 10:39. This verse tells us we are to stop focusing on ourselves and serve others.

 Romans 12:6 (NIV) says, "We have different gifts, according to the grace given to each of us."

 In 1 Peter 4:10 (NKJV), Peter wrote, "As each one has received a gift, minister it to one another, as good stewards of the manifold grace of God."

 Read Galatians 2:20. Paul shares that he lives in Christ because of what Christ did for him. His motivation to minister to others stems from that sacrifice.

If we ignore what God says in His Word, what will be the result? Well-known author, speaker, and founder of Focus on the Family, James Dobson, said in his book *Hide or Seek*, "This philosophy of 'me first' has the power to blow our world to pieces, whether applied to marriage, business, or international politics." I think he hits the nail on the head! He understands that we let our poor self-esteem and lack of concern control what we do for others.

Did you study about Copernicus in high school science? He was a man before his time. His idea about the solar system was revolutionary because he proposed that the sun was the center of the universe, not the earth. What an outlandish idea that was! It is an easy thing for us to make the mistake of thinking everything revolves around us. It is our family that is most important (and it is important). It is what we want to do that counts. It's my way, my time, my interests that dominate our decisions and behavior.

God's Word clearly states the opposite.

Are there risks in ministry?

Several families in our small Southern California church picked up children who lived in a government-subsidized apartment complex and brought them to church. It came to our attention that a single-parent mom and her daughter needed help moving into a new apartment. They had no money for the move; the mother was recovering from an illness and couldn't even clean the new place. Realizing this was an opportunity to minister, we formed a team who helped pack their belongings, move furniture, and set up the new apartment. We cleaned and unpacked the meager possessions and left feeling we had really helped the small family. Imagine our surprise when the pastor was notified that he and the church were going to be sued because of "all the damage that had happened during the move." We knew there had been no breakage or damage. Nothing came of the proposed lawsuit, but the experience made an impression on all of us. Should we continue to try to help others? Maybe we should just help our own? No, our conclusion was that we would continue to reach out when we could and share the good news about Jesus.

If you have tried to help others, you probably have encountered people who tried to take advantage of you. Do the risks of ministry outweigh the blessings? Certainly not, but they can cause us to question our effectiveness or abilities. We leap to defend our actions, but are hesitant to extend, to risk ourselves in ministry. If you are honest enough to admit you have insecurities about getting involved in ministry, what will help your self-esteem become healthier? How about a perfect role model? Would that help?

Jesus is the ultimate role model of a servant, a minister. Read Philippians 2:1–11 and find four practical insights on ministering that are found in the passage. Look for holding on to things, thinking about the person you are serving, not needing recognition and even facing rejection, and when rewards for ministry come. I hope this passage helps you find not only the reason for but also the challenge of ministry.

Are there any benefits that come from ministry?

Yes! Joy will come from ministering to others. The women mentioned in Luke 8:2–3 used their gifts and means to help support Jesus and His disciples. Surely there was joy in doing that.

Yes! Your ministry will bear fruit. You may not see it immediately, but Isaiah 55:11 tells us that God's word will not return to Him empty. Whether it was older women teaching younger ones (Titus 2:3–5) or Lydia opening her home for a church (Acts 16:40), or widows serving food and nursing the sick (1 Timothy 5:10), women's ministry efforts bore fruit.

Yes! Others will encourage you in ministry. Mary and her sister Martha were encouraged to continue their ministries by Jesus Himself (Luke 10:28–32). Paul affirmed Phoebe as a helper in and out of the church (Romans 16:1–2).

Yes! Ministry creates more opportunities for service. Priscilla's ministry lifestyle led her to teaching and establishing a home church.

Is ministry for those who have reached a certain proficiency?

Read on for my eye-opening experience related to personal ministry.

Because of a partnership between women in our states, I made a trip to Hawaii to participate in some missions projects and events. I had been asked to speak at a women's regional get-together, so my husband and I decided to expand the visit into a vacation and extend our stay on the island of Maui a week longer. I rented a condo so we were all set to have a great time on the beautiful island!

The condo couldn't have been more perfect. It was a corner unit so the views were fantastic, and my favorite part—I could hear the surf's crash!! I could tell it was going to be a very good week. After the women's event, we divided our days between doing nothing and seeing the sights. When we picked up our rental car at the airport, we were given a free upgrade. They were sorry but they had had a glitch, and we would have to take the convertible for the week. An island paradise, a blue convertible, and the surf—what could be better?

One of the things we enjoyed the most was driving randomly through the sugarcane fields. The beautiful, cloud-covered mountains formed a gorgeous backdrop for our drives. Our expeditions took us all over the island. We carried food, beverages, beach mats, towels, and folding chairs so we could stop at any scenic spot. Jan often sat in the car in the shade while I ventured out onto the sand to bask in the warm sun to the ever-present sound of crashing waves.

In our travels around the island, I saw notices about a local artisans' show. My husband wasn't interested, but every time I saw another poster, I became more determined to find the location and see the arts and Maui residents' crafts. Saturday dawned as another breathtaking day you can find only in Hawaii. There was a slight breeze for which Jan was thankful because he would be sitting in that convertible while I visited the booths.

As I approached the grassy field where the canopies were set up, I was disappointed because there was only a small

She explained that all the proceeds would go to a mission school in Latin America to provide children's school supplies.

number of displays. They were spread all over the area so the same amount of walking was involved as if there had been 20 tents. There was no breeze blowing, making it hot, and I could tell right away my vision of a fantastic foray into the arts and crafts world was going to be a short one. Good thing Jan had stayed in the car! Even though the "showing" was small, I felt obligated to visit every booth so no one felt slighted. Discouragement came quickly because I saw nothing that even remotely interested me. The items I saw did not speak to anyone's cultural heritage, and many items were actually poorly crafted.

At the end of my disappointing excursion, I noticed one more lone tent. *Should I go over there and then head to the car and the cool shade? I thought. Or, should I just call it a day and leave? Oh, you're here. Go ahead and see the last stall.* As I approached the tables under the canopy, I saw rows and rows of beautiful beaded items. Their exquisite designs simply took my breath away. There were necklaces, earrings, rings, and bracelets. The choice of colors and bead shapes worked to create pieces so unique that I wanted one of each!

My eyes flew to a particular display of bracelets made of hundreds of small beads and glass leaves. When I saw the prices, however, my heart dropped. Even as *the* vacation souvenir, I couldn't justify spending that amount. The woman operating the stall saw the gleam in my eyes as I reached for the bracelets. She must have seen, too, my eyes widen at the prices. She suggested I look at the next display stand that held simpler bracelets that had smaller price tags. We began talking about the jewelry, and I watched her as she made a necklace. She explained that all the proceeds would go to a mission school in Latin America to provide children's school supplies. Well, this changed everything! Now I felt compelled to purchase something.

One bracelet was a single band of blue-toned beads. Rather small, it had clear and blue glass leaves. It fit, and the price was something I could handle. So, it was mine. As I paid for my purchase, I heard the story behind the bracelets hanging on that particular rack. One of the young boys whose mother was making some of the jewelry asked his mother what he could do to help. She was surprised that her 12-year-old son would be interested. Thinking his interest would be short-lived, she told him she would show him how to make bracelets as his contribution to the ministry.

His designs were beautiful! He, too, could have a part in helping children go to school and have the supplies they needed to attend. If I hadn't already chosen something, that alone would have made my choice for me. I simply had to take it home with me. What a perfect illustration of the importance of personal involvement in ministry regardless of your age or ability! While this found object had a price, it was certainly unexpected, and its lesson to me was far more valuable than its price.

As I have thought about this incident, I truly believe I was led to see the craft displays because my purchase confirmed something I have believed for many years. Every believer is given the mandate to share Christ. When we establish a relationship with God's Son, we are immediately part of the "workforce" for His kingdom's work. It is easy for us to rationalize our lack of participation in fulfilling this mission by offering explanations about our life situations, which we think excuse us from being active in proclaiming the good news of Jesus. Our feelings of low self-esteem surface and influence our participation.

Although I did not meet the ministry-minded 12-year-old boy, I will remember his passion and commitment. He wasn't old enough to participate in teaching activities in Latin America or to transport supplies, but he saw that his new bead-making skills could be used to support the overseas ministry. The role models he saw in his mother's and her friends' lives motivated him to launch out and try something new. Not too many boys will step up to learn jewelry making! His example reminds me that I must take every opportunity to share my faith in Christ and minister to others in need. If my self-esteem can't handle ministry, I can equip myself to minister and use the gifts God has given me.

The Hawaiian boy's actions remind me of another 12-year-old boy whose understanding of his Father's will for his life dictated his actions. As another 12-year-old, Jesus' teaching in the Temple revealed wisdom beyond his years. He knew God had a plan for Him and He was willing to follow the path God had set for Him.

Chapter 8

When we reach the point that we listen to God's call on our lives and that He expects us to tell the world about His love, the next step is choosing how we will help fulfill the Great Commission found in Matthew 28:19–20. I have met many women who are answering God's call to minister. Just about the time I thought, *Now there's the most unique ministry I've heard*, I would meet someone else who had carved out an unusual ministry niche.

Several women in my Sunday Bible study group work with pregnant teenage girls, children who need advocates in the judicial system, and women in the adult entertainment industry. One woman and her husband counsel families in financial need and help provide aid to pay utility bills. Another group of women makes quilted blankets for hospice patients. My daughter's mother-in-law goes to the hospital's neonatal intensive care unit and rocks babies! There's a ministry for every woman just waiting for her to step beyond herself.

In our haste to do a project and move on, we often forget to involve our children and grandchildren. I recently met a mother of two young girls at a multicultural ministry orientation. As we sat talking, she told me that after our session she was taking her girls to Scoop and Scriptures, a monthly ministry of serving ice cream to residents in an adult care facility. What a simple way to include her children in ministry! She is already building up their confidence to minister.

One volunteer brought her 9-year-old granddaughter with her. After scooping ice cream, the girl told her grandmother, "Thank you for taking me. I really feel like God is calling me to do this." Can you imagine the confidence she will have as a teen, young adult, and mother in the years to come? Prepared with a healthy self-esteem and a heart for ministry!

I know I won't meet the young boy from Maui this side of heaven, but I'll never forget the model of ministry he gave me. Yes, I paid for the beaded bracelet—this found treasure—but it is another example of something rather ordinary that God has used to remind me of my responsibilities to proclaim Jesus as I walk with Him each day.

In closing, think about these words that were posted on the wall of a children's home in Calcutta, India.

> People are often unreasonable, illogical and self-centered; forgive them anyway. If you are kind, people may accuse you of selfish, ulterior motives; be kind anyway. If you are successful, you will win some false friends and some true enemies; succeed anyway. If you are honest and frank, people may cheat you; be honest and frank anyway. What you spent years building, someone could destroy overnight; build anyway. . . . The good you do today, people will often forget tomorrow; do good anyway. . . . Give the world the best you have, and it may never be enough. Give the world the best you've got anyway.
>
> —*Attributed to Mother Teresa, but now believed Kent M. Keith wrote the original version*

Found Tresure

LEGACY

AFTER RELOCATING TO THE MIDWEST, I ENJOY DRIVING through the nearby countryside. I have discovered numerous small, family cemeteries. Now, before you stop reading because you think this is a bizarre pastime, stay with me! I have found plots hidden behind split-rail fences, behind hand-built stone walls, and even in someone's front yard! My husband is now used to my shouts of, "Stop, there's a cemetery!" So he's able to make quick turns and pull off the road before we get run over. Because we live in a rural area, I've found these historic sites on country roads and nestled in out-of-the-way places. Some of them are obviously family-owned; others bear local names such as Jacobs Chapel or Plum Creek.

As we have photographed these cemeteries and some of the older headstones, we've noticed that most of them have some kind of notation that indicates something about the person's life. Many of them give clues about their occupations and how others felt about them. The terms *mother*, *grandfather*, and *wife* tell us that they left a legacy of some type to family and friends.

This really isn't too surprising because families have been doing this for centuries.

While traveling home from a missions trip to Croatia, our team had a layover in London. We only had a few morning hours to investigate the village near our hotel, so our trio started walking. Surrounding a church built in the 1600s was a graveyard. Many headstones were weathered so badly that we couldn't read their inscriptions. The ones we could decipher had the traditional comments regarding the grave's occupant. My computer photo albums preserve those memories.

I can remember touring ghost towns in Arizona and California that had mock cemeteries whose tombstones were creative and perhaps even based on real ones used during the taming of the West. An epitaph in Littleton, Colorado, says, "I told them I was sick" and makes us laugh. Professor McCracken's tombstone reads, "School is out. Teacher has gone home." Another in the Dodge City, Kansas, Boot Hill Museum is inscribed, "Here lies the body of Arkansas Jim. We made the mistake, but the joke's on him."

Serious thoughts of leaving a legacy are no laughing matter, are they? Most of us don't want to think about what people will remember about us when we leave this world. Be honest—we don't want to think that far ahead. Or, to consider that our stay on earth might end sooner than we want it to. Even though you and I aren't together physically, I can see the thoughts swirling in your mind. You are wondering what a woman's self-esteem has to do with leaving a legacy, aren't you?

Take a piece of paper and list the types of things that could be included in your epitaph. Would its words describe your profession? Or your family relationships? Would it attest to what you accomplished in life? Would there be any mention of your spiritual journey?

We've already considered the impact that self-esteem has on recognizing our abilities, on our communication, our relationships, how (or if) we share Christ with others, and our attitude toward ministry. It should be no surprise, then, that poor self-esteem will influence our legacy negatively. I'm not saying that you won't achieve your goals and make worthy contributions to your company or be remembered for nurturing in your family. I am saying, however, that your life might not have the joy and contentment possible when you realize you are valuable in God's eyes.

Sometimes my greatest goal for today is to survive it! Have you ever felt that way? As we move through a blur of days and weeks trying to meet our families' needs and fulfill some personal dreams, it is difficult to focus on what our long-term influence will be. We work outside the home; we work inside the home; and we chauffeur kids back and forth to school, soccer games, and piano lessons. We may carve out time to volunteer at the middle school as a library worker or hand out bottles of cold water in Jesus' name at the annual community harvest festival.

There's something I am *not* saying here. I am not hinting that when we participate in community projects, missions trips, or teach children in Vacation Bible School, we are doing it for recognition or self-promotion. That is not to be our motive for seeking to influence others. The legacies you and I leave are to be ones that bring glory to God's name. Our motivation should be pure and selfless. I learned something from a found object about a person's legacy. The end result of the research I did wasn't what I thought it would be.

I have always been fascinated with old houses. Every time our family moved, I would drive around until I found the old part of town. One such town was established in the late 1800s and was a virtual picture book of old houses replete with gingerbread trim and turrets. While living there I never missed the December home tour. I never owned one of these older beauties, but I certainly spent a lot of time dreaming about how I would refurbish one!

The town where our children were born had street after street of large houses whose stories filled numerous books. I worked at the public library in those days and had access to files full of photographs of the area in its heyday. Some were actual mansions that were owned by famous people from the East. Al Capone was said to have lived in one of them. Harold Bell Wright, author of *Shepherd of the Hills*, lived in a carriage house behind a huge Spanish-style home complete with a basement bowling alley. I must admit I had some flights of fancy regarding many of these residences!

After living out of state in two large cities for ten years for several years, we returned to live in a small Southern California town that had its share of old places too. Because we were unfamiliar with the area, we chose to rent for the first year. The elderly woman who rented to us owned several properties in town. As we settled into her former home, we got to know her and discovered that she owned an old house I had longed to see inside. She wanted to renovate the house and make it ready for renters. I wanted to live there, but it wasn't suitable for a family with two teenagers. Because my husband had been a property manager in the past, she asked him to oversee the renovation. So began our journey with one of the lovelies of years past.

Nestled in an orange grove, the 1906 dwelling was constructed in the mission style popular in Southern California. Its wide veranda porch wrapped around two sides of the house. The inside was a decorator's paradise with hardwood floors and built-in china cabinets. The formal dining room had dark wood panels below dark brown leather wallpaper. The upstairs was a master suite waiting to happen with enough room for a walk-in closet room, a study, and large bath. As the renovation began in earnest, my husband and our oldest son spent hours doing the things they could do—painting the wrought iron fence, tearing out kitchen cabinets, and painting walls. My husband hired a craftsman to do the kitchen remodel. The owner decided to leave the existing downstairs bath intact and just update its look with new hardware and light fixtures.

There, on the bottom, written in dark pencil strokes was the name George Clemens. *I only knew one Clemens—Samuel Clemens—better known as Mark Twain, the author of the classic* The Adventures of Huckleberry Finn.

This was the room that held a surprise for me! We were doing the final cleaning after the renovations were almost finished. The large drawers in a built-in wall unit had been removed, and I was putting them back in when I turned one over. There, on the bottom, written in dark pencil strokes was the name *George Clemens.* I only knew one Clemens—Samuel Clemens—better known as

Mark Twain, the author of the classic *The Adventures of Huckleberry Finn*. I immediately began investigating why George Clemens's name was on the bottom of a drawer in a house in Southern California. The owner told me that the house had been built for Samuel Clemens's sister, Rose, by their brother. What a find! True, I had never heard of George, but his brother is legendary. His books are still on high school required reading lists.

I have since learned that Clemens's brother's name was not George and that evidently the house was built for someone else's "Rose." So, back to researching I went! I discovered that one of Clemens's daughters was named Jean and that she had epilepsy. In those days very little was known about the disease so she was institutionalized as part of her care. While reading a murder mystery one day, I found her name and the title of a book about carved treasure chests. Evidently, Jean learned to carve as part of her therapy while in a sanitarium for her illness. Originally, I had begun to weave a scenario about Samuel Clemens's daughter who was a wood carver because of the influence of her Uncle George, who was a woodworker too. A great scenario, but an inaccurate one! In all of my research, I found nothing to substantiate my theories. It made for good storytelling, though, just as the original tale I'd been given.

Regardless of the real story behind the signature on the bathroom drawer, the autograph of the woodworker was a found object. It wasn't something I could take with me, but its discovery illustrated for me the lasting impression certain people make on us. Musicians change their world with new compositions and musical styles. Artists are recognized for new techniques, which are studied over and over again. Architects design buildings that are heralded for their innovations. Technology has been revolutionized by individuals whose creative efforts take the average person to worlds they never dreamed of before. Legacies left by these people live on past their lifetimes, continuing to influence future generations in small and large ways.

I cannot honestly say that George Clemens influenced my life, but I can say that I have thought about my discovery many times. So, maybe my thinking changed a bit? It became part of the entire process of the old house's beautification. The bathroom design and its built-ins remained well past the builder's lifetime. Now, we all leave legacies. The pertinent question is, What kind of legacies do we leave? People we want to look up to may destroy their reputations because of dishonesty, broken promises, or failure to live up to God's standards.

None of us consciously seeks to leave a tarnished legacy, one that makes people think unsavory thoughts or have negative reactions when our names are mentioned. On the contrary, we want to be remembered for the positive things we did. Confucius, a fifth-century BC Chinese teacher, editor, and philosopher, said this about planning for the future and investing in others: "If you think in terms of a year, plant a seed. If in terms of ten years, plant trees. If in terms of one hundred years, teach the people." This is certainly true, isn't it?

You are a leader in some area of your life, and you have the opportunity to leave a strong legacy. Because others have had an impact on my leadership life, I have tried to justify their investment of time and energy and lead in such a way that I help women to develop their skills. As we mentor novice leaders, consistency is a critical element in all we do. The term *wishy-washy* is not one that any leader wants someone to use in describing them! Part of leaving a sound legacy is a stable, consistent approach to problem solving. If we don't exhibit consistency in our planning, organization, and approach, we won't be the kind of role model we should be. Our effectiveness will be diminished, and the legacy we leave will not be as strong as it should be.

Some of you who are reading this have just skipped over this part about leadership legacies. I know you have! You've skimmed over these last few sentences because you don't consider yourself a leader in any capacity. And you're wrong! You don't have to lead a board of directors of a large corporation to be considered a leader. Directing a successful county supervisor's election campaign doesn't count any more than leading your children or grandchildren to understand that God loves them. Hosting a neighborhood ladies' coffee demonstrates you are interested in others, as a leader should be. Holding a fancy title doesn't make you a leader!

As I have researched Samuel Clemens's family and life, there is no doubt about the legacy he left as a world-renowned author. He wrote novels, nonfiction, essays, and short stories. He was a nationally known humorist whose works have endured the test of time. If George Clemens had in fact been Jean's uncle, would his influence have extended to decisions she made? Could his preferences, attitudes, and behavior have impacted how she lived her life? Even though I couldn't connect Samuel Clemens to George Clemens and the story I was told, my research wasn't wasted. As I read and followed leads, I realized how influential individuals can be in our lives.

In the same way Clemens's literary legacy influences us today, so do the legacies of countless women in the past who have displayed notable Christian hospitality, grace, and commitment. Just like us, they were women of all ages, some single and some married, coming from different social and economic standings and various educational backgrounds. They left legacies that inspire and motivate us to use our God-given abilities in our families, communities, and churches.

I imagine you could quickly name women who have left a legacy that has inspired you. Perhaps your own mother demonstrated how to love unconditionally. Other women in your family may have left legacies of personal strength, overcoming difficult circumstances, or examples of unfailing faith in God. Have you ever made a list of women whose legacy has impacted your life? Why not do that right now? If any of them are still living, this would be a great time to contact them and tell them how much they have meant to you.

Legacies cannot all be in the past, however. How do we make sure we leave a legacy that is strong, one that will stand the test of time? I think there are four things we should keep in mind as we renew our determination to influence others, maybe even beyond our lives here on earth.

- We need to be *intentional*. This intentionality should include the skills we develop, the attitudes we perhaps need to change, and the behavior we show. In essence, every area of our lives needs to be viewed in light of our influence. Leave nothing to chance; a strong legacy is not happenstance.

- Having a *long view* is something else we should think about. We can't let the future "take care of itself" while we change the beds, cook lasagna, and go back and forth to work. If we feel inadequate as wives, mothers, neighbors, co-workers, or church leaders and members, we need to find ways to grow toward a healthier self-esteem so we will be more confident in influencing others.

- Whether you are a team leader at work or serve on your church's hospitality committee, you should be interested in *equipping other leaders*. It is easy to become trapped in getting the immediate done and then moving on to the next project. When we fail to equip others, our legacies will be short-lived.

- How do you feel when your boss compliments you on your work for a new client? Do you feel an inner glow for a job well done? When your pastor affirms what the youth teachers did at youth camp, does your breath catch a little because you were part of the effort and know students' lives were changed? Now apply that feeling to others. Being an *encourager* helps build others' self-esteem so they can reach their God-given potential. Encouraging others helps them utilize their gifts and abilities. Remember the story about the girl helping her grandmother scoop ice cream? That grandmother is leaving a legacy that shouts personal involvement in ministry. In turn, her example is instilling that you-can-do-it mentality, something her granddaughter will never forget.

In my mind's eye, I can still see George Clemens's signature on the bottom of that bathroom cabinet drawer. It was a large scrawl, one that no doubt was written with pride. As far as I know, it is still there today, but it may never see the light of day again! The drawer will always serve as a reminder that my legacy must be stable. I need to be faithful to godly principles that will remain long after I have left this life.

Women who have healthy self-esteem are more likely to leave a legacy that will speak to a faithful walk with God, compassion for others, and a desire to salt her world with the knowledge of the Light of the world.

Chapter 9

Found Treasure

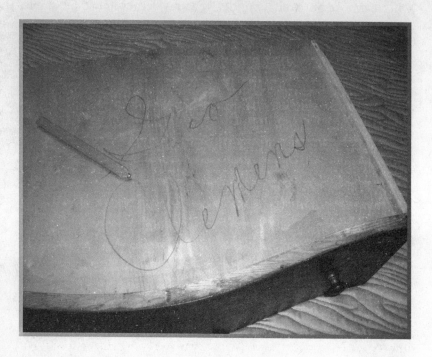

CHAPTER 10

NOT FOR THE FAINT OF HEART

IN A NUTSHELL, MY MOTHER'S MOTHER WAS AN unusual woman! This says a lot about her life: I never lived near her, but she still had a huge influence on my life. I guess a lot of people would say the same thing about their grandmothers. As in most families, I heard many stories about her childhood and married life. (I think it's a grandmother's job to pass on family heritage, so get with it, gals!) Even with all her storytelling, I was unprepared for what I found one day while going through some of her things after her death.

My grandmother, Graney to my brother and me, was not a wealthy woman; well, that is not quite accurate. She was born into a well-to-do family late in her parents' lives. She was the youngest daughter in a rural Texas family. She arrived after the long-awaited and only boy, so she always believed she was an afterthought of her parents. Her sisters were grown and married by the time she appeared on the scene. Some of the wealth that should have come her way when her mother died was taken by her sisters. She always told us that the only things she got from her mother were an etched water jug and matching glass and a china soup tureen.

Her dolls and other childhood possessions were destroyed in the proverbial house fire.

One photograph I have is of Graney as a teenager and shows her standing next to a friend seated at a piano. She is wearing a long, white dress made of what was called cotton lawn fabric. On her arm is a wide gold-plated bracelet that speaks to some affluence in her day. The photograph must have been taken prior to her mother's death and the fire because the scene seems to show a more privileged lifestyle. The bracelet survived the fire and the multiple moves from Texas to Arizona and around that state. One year for Christmas, my mother gave me the bracelet, which I keep in a special spot in my jewelry box. I wear the bracelet only on special occasions. It is a reminder that Graney was a determined woman and a woman who was strong in the face of adversity.

My grandmother's upbringing did not prepare her for the circumstances of life that were to come. Indeed, who of us is truly prepared for what God allows into our lives? After marriage, she and my grandfather moved to Arizona where he eventually was employed by the Civilian Conservation Corps (CCC). Granddaddy always said he was preparing young men for war as he trained them to operate large machinery. He was correct. When World War II came, many of the men he taught became tank drivers and machinists.

Living through the Great Depression brought stories of deprivation and uncertainty, and my family was no exception. One of those events occurred at Christmastime when the small family of four was living in a motel room while my grandfather was trying to find work. Graney knew there would be no Christmas gifts that year under the tree. In fact, there was no tree! Christmas Eve came and my mother and her younger brother went to sleep knowing that the next day would be a shadow of former years' celebrations. Graney said she possessed two things of value—her gold-plated bracelet and a watch her father had given to her on her 16th birthday. She gave these two items to her children so that Christmas Day would dawn with one gift for each of them. My brother now has the watch, and I have the bracelet. (My mother ended up with the watch when her brother was killed at the end of World War II, and she passed it on to my brother.) Graney was not a woman who willingly succumbed to difficult circumstances. Her life, like many others', was not for the faint of heart!

Life became even more uncertain for Graney when my grandfather was killed in an automobile accident when I was 2 years old. His death threw her into a life of financial desperation as she sought to make a livelihood just to survive. After making her living from crocheting items for a year, she finally found employment doing alterations for a local department store. (Can you imagine trying to make a living crocheting and selling the pieces?) Then another blow fell when my mother's only brother was killed when an air force airplane crashed. Ironically, he had reenlisted to help her financially. Now, he, too, was gone, and she was left with just my mother who was living in Texas at the time.

On the box's embossed lid was a picture of a beautifully dressed woman with flowers and peacocks around her. As I lifted the box lid to see the contents, I gasped out loud.

Graney's world became only a fraction of what it had once been. As she struggled to make sense of the whys concerning all that happened, she remained faithful to God and her belief that He would take care of her and be the solace she needed. She was an active member of her Baptist church and worked with young women in missions groups. She loved to plan programs and encourage the women to learn about and pray for missionaries. She might have been limited financially, but her world vision was still strong.

As I was going through her things after Graney passed away, I found a beautifully decorated box that was obviously old. On the box's embossed lid was a picture of a beautifully dressed woman with flowers and peacocks around her. As I lifted the box lid to see the contents, I gasped out loud, for there nestled in the bottom of the box, was a 24-inch length of bright red hair! I haven't said that Graney's hair was what used to be called carrot-top red. She never liked the color of her hair, as she thought it restricted the colors of clothing she could wear. She felt she always had to wear blues and lavenders. No reds, pinks, or oranges were ever found in her closet! Where in the world had this found object come from? I asked my mother, and the story she told me is how I have come to think of Graney.

My grandmother had worn her hair long for most of her life, as was the style in those days. My grandfather usually spent his annual vacation hunting. One weekend when he announced plans to go hunting, it was not well received by Graney. She told him that if he persisted in going hunting, she would cut her hair! Why that particular threat was made, I don't know. I remember my mother telling me my grandfather had always loved her long hair. Perhaps he didn't believe she would go through with her threat, so he went hunting. What I had found in that beautiful box was the fulfillment of her promise! The box remained in her possession until her death, some 45 years later. I'll never know why she had kept her hair, but I assume that it represented her determination to follow through on what she committed to do!

I packed up my found object and kept it with other mementos for many years, moving it from house to house, state to state. At one point I made plans to have the hair made into doll wigs and give a porcelain doll to each of my children as a keepsake memento of their great-grandmother. Their response was unanimous, *No way!* Well, I couldn't think of any other way to use the hair, so not long ago I decided the contents of the beautiful box had made its last move. I kept the box, but Graney's hair was left behind. If anyone found the locks of hair I discarded, it wouldn't have been for the faint of heart!

I was never able to live near my grandmother. She lived in Arizona, and we moved around in Texas, from Texas to California, and back to Texas before we ended up in California in time for me to graduate from high school and begin college. We always made at least one trip to see her every year and often two, no matter where we lived. Since she was completely alone, except for kind neighbors and her church family, we spent numerous Christmas holidays in her small southeastern Arizona town. The summers we traveled to see her were the worst. Do you know how hot it gets in Arizona? Graney didn't have air conditioning, and I would lie awake listening to the neighborhood dogs bark until the desert air cooled the house down a bit so I could sleep.

I had a pastor who described one of his first houses as "so small you had to go outside to change your mind!" Graney's house was just like that. Everything seemed to be miniature—a small kitchen with tiny dining room attached to a miniscule living room. Two bedrooms barely big enough for double beds and one bathroom so small you had to go . . . well, you get the idea.

I mentioned that Graney was very active in her church, and I suspect she wouldn't have made it through the tragic events of losing her husband and son if the church family hadn't been there to support her through those dark days. She could have let her circumstances paralyze her, but she chose to pick up the pieces of her life and move forward. I never talked to her about how she was able to do the things she did. I regret now that I didn't ask her how she got the alteration job, or how she marketed her crocheted pieces. I suspect she would have said, "I did what I had to." Like many other women during those years, she didn't have a formal education. She had not been trained to do anything. At one time she wanted to be a nurse, but her parents objected, so that was that. Graney never learned to drive, so even getting to the job she now had to have was difficult. She managed that too—she walked back and forth!

Like I said, I don't believe Graney was that different from other widows who were forced to leave home to work, who lost sons in the war, or who lived alone. She was different, however, when viewed from what she accomplished in spite of these difficult circumstances. It wasn't an outgoing personality that made her strong. She must have been afraid during those early years of widowhood as she had to maintain her home, make a living, and do many things she'd never done before. Where did she get her courage? She relied on God's strength and guidance to help her make decisions. But, aside from that, did her actions speak to that saying "not for the faint of heart"? Her self-confidence—her self-esteem—was stronger than her grief and uncertainty.

So, think about this a minute: What part does fear play in your life? Be honest! Does it paralyze you and keep you from doing what you should do? Is fear's grip on you so strong that your self-esteem is damaged? *So, she's found something else I need to work on!* you may be thinking. And, you are right. I really believe that we let fear dominate our lives too much. It affects our ability to make good decisions; it hampers our trying to do new things. Fear can keep us from sharing Christ, and it can control our relationships.

Make a list of four life situations that you've had where fear stymied your actions (or could have but didn't). Under each one write what you did in reaction to the fear. Did the situation and fear control you? Or did you work through them building a healthier self-esteem as a result? Here are three examples of what I'm talking about.

SCENARIO 1

You need a better job with more pay and benefits! Your employer has posted a position that you think you can handle but feel there's no point in applying because the position requires a college degree, and you didn't finish your senior year. Is fear present in this situation? How can you handle this?

🙜 SCENARIO 2 🙛

Your neighbor is one of the most difficult persons you've ever met! She is the "watchdog" type and always criticizes your children. You know you need to talk to her to clear the air, but fear keeps you from approaching her. Now what?

🙜 SCENARIO 3 🙛

You are interested in a ministry project for women in your church. You have some ideas but you are hesitant to voice them. You whisper to yourself, "Oh, never mind. I'm too busy anyway." Is fear lurking around the corner?

Can you see fear rearing its head in these situations? You've heard the saying about lemons, right? There are days when I think that's all I bring home from the grocery store! I open the kitchen cabinet and lemons spill out. The refrigerator bins are full of lemons. Even the pantry has a box of dried lemons. You've probably had days like mine. While we know the rest of the saying about making lemonade, we just can't muster the energy or courage to do anything about our situation. Fear takes over our thinking, and it just isn't in us to climb the mountain. Our self-esteem isn't healthy enough to overcome the things that we fear—financial troubles, marital conflict, depression, work-related stress, or whatever else.

When our life situations, whether of our making or not, damage our self-esteem, we become less effective at home, at work, or in our spiritual journey. The Bible is not silent on the topic of fear. Second Timothy 1:7 (NKJV) says, "For God has not given us a spirit of fear, but of power and of love and of a sound mind." Isaiah commented, "So do not fear, for I am with you" (Isaiah 41:10 NIV).

When I began writing this chapter, I remembered a book I bought several years ago when I was taking a course for my master's degree. I met the author, so I have a special connection and have found it a valuable resource. *The Counsel of a Friend* by Lynda D. Elliott is a great source for anyone who has friends who need some help with various issues. Who doesn't have friends with needs? Elliott constructed her book by topic and supports her statements with biblical references, making it a great tool for easy reference.

How do we get caught in fear? Sometimes we are fearful because we develop habits that stem from what we learned in our families. Did you grow up hearing, "Be careful" and "Don't try that"? Living a life full of warnings can make us hesitant to take steps toward new beginnings, finding solutions to our dilemmas, or making decisions that require a certain measure of courage. If a woman goes through life with others making important decisions for her, she never develops the skills that will help her deal with normal life issues, not to mention the crises every woman faces at one time or another.

Satan is delighted when a Christian woman is unable to experience the full measure of God's love. She will never be content and have the peace only He gives. When fear keeps us from being all God wants us to be, hinders us from achieving our goals and dreams within God's plan, harms our relationships, and demoralizes our perception of ourselves, we need to find ways to face and overcome the fear. I've mentioned before that I'm kind of a bottom-line, results-oriented person, so I think having an action plan could help you loosen the hold fear has on your life.

1. Pray for God to guide you as you take steps toward breaking out of fear's control.

2. Review what you've already done about your situation.

3. Is God leading you to do something you haven't done yet?

4. Make a list of things you can do that you haven't done yet.

5. Use a Bible dictionary or concordance and look up verses under "fear not." Write out a brief summary of each passage. Begin with these: Proverbs 3:5–8; Psalm 103; Isaiah 27:3–4; Matthew 6:25–34; and Philippians 4:6–9.

6. Be thankful. God will work in your life!

7. Be informed.

8. Wait in peace.

As I look at the box that held my grandmother's shorn hair all those years, I think about what she meant to me. She sewed an entire school year's wardrobe for me when I was in the eighth grade. When I was confined to bed with mononucleosis for six months, she sent me notes, letters, jokes, magazines, and even baby-doll pajamas to lift my spirits. She taught me how to crochet. She was right-handed, but taught me to do it left-handed. (That's a story in itself!) I loved looking at her miniature pitcher collection on a shelf in her dining room. They were from all over the world, given to her by her son's air force buddies. But, these are just memories and "things." What she left me is more important. She was an example of what it means to be courageous. She stepped through life even though her footsteps were laden with grief. Facing uncertainty, she conquered her circumstances with determination and the assurance that God had not abandoned her.

Perhaps you can visualize Graney's hair lying in that box—those carrot-red tresses of the woman who stood her ground—and as you reflect on the issues in your own life that challenge your self-esteem. As you move away from fear toward a healthier self-esteem, remember that life is not for the faint of heart. Lynda D. Elliott states in her book *The Counsel of a Friend*, "Only knowing God and experiencing His love can cause us to feel secure. The shed blood of Jesus grants us security now and forever."

Found Treasure

CHAPTER 11

PIECE BY PIECE

THERE LAY THE TATTERED OLD QUILT—ON THE ground in a heap. It had obviously been tossed there as an afterthought, most likely to save someone a trip to the trash bin nearby. At one time, it must have been a source of pride to someone, but the quilt was now only a shadow of its former self. A casual glance told me it hadn't been used on a bed for a long time. Its original purpose of bringing warmth and comfort had long been cast aside.

Instead of providing a sense of security or displaying the quilter's skill, the old quilt was covered with hardened drops of burgundy paint. The patches that were free from paint had spots of long-standing mildew. In other words, the quilt was not worth anything to anyone. No one, that is, except me. While my personal forays into the quilting world have been very limited, I have always admired the skill, artistry, and attention to detail that are part of quilts. My quilting experiences have revolved around concern that the quilt pattern did not require point matching or intricate cutting. Straight lines with no triangles are what I look for!

Since the old quilt had led such an obviously hard life, I felt I had to rescue it. I seemed to be the only one remotely interested in its survival, so surely my offer to purchase it would be met with a positive response. When I approached the woman in charge of the sales, she said I could have the quilt for ten cents. *What a treasure I've found!* What a terrible comedown for a piece that had no doubt been lovingly crafted. *Ten cents?* It took me just a moment to gather it into my arms and trundle to the car. At that point I didn't have any thoughts as to how I could use the quilt, but since when had my purchases of old objects met a "useable" clause? With a sense of "rescue justification," I left with the quilt safely stowed in the backseat of my car. I would worry later about how I would use it.

My appreciation of quilts is part of my heritage. My mother's mother (Graney) was a quilter, and I have several of her projects. Her quilts were not original patterns and certainly wouldn't fall into the categories of the works of art mentioned in the popular author's "Elm Creek Quilters" series. Using bought patterns, she stitched to make something useful as well as beautiful. She made wedding quilts for both my brother and me. She was still alive when I married, but my brother received his quilt many years after her death, when he found his bride.

My quilt collection includes some beautiful examples of the craft, which were given to me by a very good friend whose mother had made them. When the friend went into a retirement facility, she didn't have room for them and knew I would value and cherish them. So I became the delighted recipient of three old quilts made with loving hands. I have one quilt, in the Double Wedding Ring pattern, made for me by my mother-in-law.

When we lived in Colorado, she would quilt as my father-in-law drove their camper from California to visit us each year. She was understandably proud of her quilting stitches—12 to an inch. The stitches were so small that they were almost invisible. She quilted until the onset of Alzheimer's, and I regret that I do not have more of her handiwork.

It was probably because of these connections to quilts that I felt the urge to salvage some part of the derelict bedcover I found that day. When I unloaded the unfortunate remnant, I questioned again how in the world I'd use it. I could tell by looking that repair and restoration weren't options. Neither was displaying the quilt like the one I hung in the stairway leading to the second story of our home. The only feasible option would be salvaging sections and repurposing them.

Repurposing is a popular term right now. Reality shows document two friends who scour the countryside for anything that can be used for household decor. Old industrial light fixtures are turned into floor lamps. Warehouse carts become coffee tables, and discarded furniture is cut down, refinished, and used as accent tables and kitchen storage units. As I spread out the old quilt, I discovered to my dismay that there was not a single piece without paint or mildew larger than a few square inches. Now I faced a dilemma. Had I rescued the quilt only to be the one who finally threw it away? There wasn't even a piece large enough to make a pillow!

Please understand that cutting up a quilt is something I had never done. Even frayed edges weren't reason enough to destroy a handmade object. But, the reality was that this was simply the only viable option if any part of the quilt was to be saved. I began to plot how I could cut the quilt to net the largest pieces possible. As I pinned and repinned, measured and remeasured, I saw that the largest piece with no paint drops or mildew was only about eight square inches. I took a deep breath and began to cut away the frayed, threadbare spots while at the same time avoiding the paint and mildew spots.

When I finished, I saw only the remains—a virtual patchwork within a quilt pattern. There were gaps, holes, frayed edges, and dangling threads in abundance. To one side was the small pile of "whole, usable" pieces—about six of them. Not a very noble ending for a once-beautiful example of textile art. I have to admit to a moment of depression when I placed the unsalvageable remains in the trash. Now my task was to take what was left and do something worthwhile with the few pieces I had saved.

I've thought about that quilt through the years, especially when I look at my other quilts that are still intact and useable. The fact that the quilt's beauty had been destroyed by mistreatment and neglect was bad enough, but I keep seeing the holes, the gaps. I am not a knitter but I've heard stories of finishing a project only to discover a dropped stitch. A dropped stitch makes a hole in the knitted piece. It might not be noticeable at first glance, but to the experienced knitter it flashes like a neon sign. Isn't life a lot like this?

Just as the old quilt had many pieces and when stitched together made the whole, our lives have many dimensions.

One area of many women's lives is work. Because of financial needs, or because they want to, many women work outside their homes. Some are fortunate to work at home. Do *not* think that I am saying we have to leave the house to work! I was a homemaker until all my children left home except for temporary and part-time jobs. In fact, believe that the idea of being either a homemaker or a working woman is completely off base. Women who are employed outside the home are still homemakers, right? It isn't an either/or situation. But, that's another topic.

Just as the old quilt had many pieces and when stitched together made the whole, our lives have many dimensions, and for a lot of us the workplace is one of those life segments. The landscape of women in the workplace has changed dramatically over the years. Societal movements have had an impact on the issues surrounding whether women should work, where they could work, whether their pay would be equal to men's, job discrimination, . . . and the list goes on. Women entered the workforce doing things they had never done before. Debates raged and the stage was set for identity crises.

Women may feel guilty for leaving children in child care, leaving the housework undone (there is some virtue in this, however!), leaving their homes for long periods of time, leaving volunteer work for others to do. A lot of leaving takes place! Not long ago, 34 percent of American households had a single-parent mother as sole supporter. With shifts and change, many of us have suffered ups and downs in our self-esteem. We have grappled with piecing together our family and personal "quilts" in order to achieve balance, security, and contentment.

Look at these 2010 census statistics, according to the US Department of Labor:

- Of 123 million women in the US, 72 million are in the workforce or looking for work.
- Seventy-three (73) percent of these women work full time.
- Twenty-seven (27) percent of them work part-time.
- Women earn 81 percent of men's salaries.
- The higher a woman's education, the higher likelihood she will work outside the home.
- Single women spent 25.4 percent of their income on shelter.
- A higher percentage of women at age 23 had bachelor's degrees than men of the same age.

If you have a few spare minutes some day (no, that's not meant as a joke), search the Internet to learn about working women and self-esteem. For example, Women's Media: Expert Advice for Business Women has numerous articles on the subject, two of which I found especially interesting. Whether a woman works outside her home or starts her own home business, she will usually face some self-esteem issues as she strives for productivity, advancement, and balance. Suzanne Harrill addresses self-esteem in an article entitled, "How Do You Feel about Yourself? Recognizing Signs of High and Low Self-Esteem."

Harrill asserts that self-empowerment, good relationships, and satisfaction at work are the foundation of healthy work self-esteem. She lists these things as evidences of high self-esteem. Read them over and see if they apply to you at work.

- Self-control.
- Dependence on others.
- Balance of thoughts.
- Listen to others' points of view.
- Respect differences between people.
- Know own strengths and weaknesses.
- Know difference between being and doing.

That's a pretty good list, isn't it?

OK, here's a second list. If we want our self-esteem at work to be healthy, we need to be aware of the signs of low self-esteem and make changes while being true to ourselves, effective for God, and capable in our work performance. Look at these and see what you think.

- Being an overachiever.
- Criticizing others frequently.
- Playing the victim.
- Engaging in self-blame.
- Having a need to always be right.
- Taking over others' responsibilities.
- Comparing yourself to others.
- Using lots of "shoulds," "oughts," and "could haves" in conversations.

Did you see yourself in any of these indicators?

You may have started your own business. Perhaps you work for a health insurance company. You may do the billing hours for a law firm. You could be the CEO of a distributing company or the district buyer for a chain of department stores. Women are in virtually every field of employment. Some of the time, we are doing things we really enjoy. Other days it's almost more than we can do to get up, get ready, and leave the house to face a sticky situation fraught with tension at the office. Our self-esteem, whether we realize it or not, is directly tied to how we view the work in our lives.

Many women in the workforce feel as if they don't have any options. They must work. They may be overloaded with responsibilities due to downsizing in the workplace. They feel they have to put up with extremely difficult bosses or sticky conditions because they have to have a paycheck. Tensions and conflicts at work are the norm rather than the exception, and the stress of work goes home with them every day. These issues can undermine a woman's self-esteem because she can't view herself as part of a solution—just someone caught in a never-ending cycle of unrest, uncertainty, and uneasiness. When we face these work situations, we all feel helpless, but that is when a mentor, adviser, life coach, and God Himself can guide us through the storm.

As you stitch the work portion of your quilt, you might find it helpful to ask yourself some questions. Some of them will bother you. You may think I'm being nosy to even ask them! I believe, however, that if you can answer them honestly, you will move closer to developing a healthy work self-esteem; and when that happens, your overall perception of yourself, your contributions, and your value will increase, making you more contented and confident to look for God's working in your life.

So, here are the questions. If you journal, you might want to jot down your responses so you can review them six months from now. It could be interesting!

- Is prestige important to you?
- Do you perform at work to gain esteem?
- Do you feel guilty that you are not expending enough effort to do your job?
- Do you feel pressure to do more?
- Do you require continual motivation from your boss?
- Are you afraid to try something new?
- Do you do things just to secure your job?
  Is job security important?
- Do you feel restricted?
- Are you overcome by regulations?
- Do you frequently disagree with your boss?
- How important is winning to you?
- Do you have to have others' recognition?
- Do you go out of your way to gain rewards?
- Is your performance related to effort?
- How do you feel when you finish a task?
- Do you set goals?

Women have been regarded as the "kin keepers" for their families. We knit, crochet, and quilt the fabrics of our family lives together. We may even call or write our husband's relatives to keep them up-to-date as he never gets around to it. We strive to keep relationships healthy and to repair the gaps that conflict and misunderstandings can create. It doesn't take long to find out that the fabrics of our society are frayed and that there are holes caused by neglect and abuse. Children in many homes just grow up rather than being reared by loving parents. Youth go through their teenage years with no guidance or encouragement and fall into those gaps and become the dropped stitches of society. These issues can damage relationships and families. The workplace is another arena where women strive to bridge gaps, resolve conflict, smooth the waters, and find satisfaction in what they do.

Being in the workforce can be an opportunity for us as women to help build others' self-esteem. I'm afraid that we are often so concerned about ourselves and our perception of things as they relate to us, that we neglect the things we can do to make a difference in someone else's life. Can you take one more list? Try one or two of these things and watch another person's self-esteem bloom.

- Give them your attention.
- Show your appreciation and gratitude when appropriate.
- Don't criticize or ridicule them in front of others.
- Listen attentively.
- Demonstrate acceptance and approval.
- Don't argue.

I remember my oldest son's first girlfriend. Her parents were divorced, and she had little contact with her father. She had one younger brother and was in charge of his care before and after school while their mother worked. Working was a necessity for Mom, but that left this teen on her own much of the time. She often walked to our house after school. One day my son came into the room where I sat reading and told me his friend had a question to ask me. My alarm antennae went up! "Of course," I replied. I was completely surprised by her question: "I've torn the hem of my skirt. Could you show me how to fix it?" She had "mended" it with the household stapler. I got a needle and thread and showed her how to put in a hem.

Several weeks later there was a follow-up report on this girl's newly developed skill. She came to our house again (my cookies were definitely not what drew her!) and proudly showed me the hem she had put in on a pair of pants. One small issue: she couldn't find any sewing thread so she had used all six strands of a length of embroidery thread to do the stitching! I have thought about this experience many times because it reminds me of the gaps created by our failures to nurture, teach, and encourage those in our spheres of influence. Neglect is like the mildew stains on my old, discarded quilt. Its presence damages the fabric strength.

God created us with the ability to see the needs of our families, friends, and yes, even co-workers. Our relationships with others should result in bonds created by our love and concern. When we as parents miss opportunities to teach life lessons, fail to bring up our children in the "nurture and admonition of the Lord," and let "what happens, happen," we are just like the dried paint blobs on the quilt I found that day. When we, as women in the workplace, neglect to bring God into our relationships with others—at work in this instance—this weakens the fabric of His divine purpose, causing holes and frayed edges.

A woman's self-esteem is connected to the work she does and is an important area of her life. It will affect other areas of her life because she can't turn work "off" when she leaves her desk, the computer, inventories, projects, or the classroom. We need to be honest in our appraisal of the work we do and determine if our self-esteem is healthy in the workplace. If it isn't, we should take the steps to make it healthier and not let problems escalate.

Did I ever find a use for the quilt's remnants? Actually, I did! I used several pieces to make small stuffed shapes—hearts, birds, etc.—and combined them with bath salts, soaps, and lotions in gift baskets. I made some pincushions and sold them in a home decor store I owned at the time. One particular piece was very attractive and still had good color, so I made a miniature quilt embellishing it with old buttons. It rests in the arms of a small stuffed bear in an antique Irish cupboard we use as an entertainment center. The miniature quilt serves as a reminder that, just like anything else, quilts need to be cared for. Our lives are no different—they require loving care, attention, and God's direction to make us the beautiful and useful creations He intends us to be. And that includes our work!

Found Treasure

NOT JUST ONE MIRACLE

WELL, IT SEEMS I HAVE LED YOU TO CONSIDER A variety of issues that relate to women and their self-esteem. God's Word supports His attitude toward us and His love for us. How can our self-esteem *not* grow when we see Him at work? I had an experience as I was writing this that illustrates this.

At a coffee shop one day, I visited the restroom before settling down to work on my computer. As I entered, I heard a woman's voice ask, "Are you a woman there?" I can only assume she'd met a man in the restroom one time! I responded with a hesitant, "Yes." She then proceeded to tell part of her personal story to me through the wall of the restroom stall. She had lost one of her kidneys as a result of 20 years of negligent medical care. She made the comment, "I guess God wasn't through with me yet because here I am. I'm sorry . . . you really probably don't want to hear all of this." Assuring her I was an interested listener, I told her that I believe God spared her life so that she could tell others her story and maybe help them by her testimony to His goodness and mercy.

What do you do when difficult times come? Notice I didn't use the word *if*. Difficulties are (or will be) a very real part of all

One day I noticed an envelope glued to the inside back cover—a found treasure! I eagerly opened this to find a brief, typed letter. The postmark and date on the letter indicated it had been written in 1979.

of our lives, so we must be prepared to handle them within our limited understanding even though our emotions and spirit are in turmoil. That doesn't mean we will fly through any tragedy or traumatic circumstance unscathed, but if we have in our arsenal God's lasting principles, we will at least realize we can rely on Him to guide us and comfort us. In *The Counsel of a Friend*, author Lynda Elliott says, "Keep your mind girded up with God's Word on an ongoing basis. Fill your mind during the easier times so you will be able to more readily recall it during difficulties." This is insightful advice!

My father enjoyed reading Scripture in the Amplified Bible. He liked this version because it often clarifies specific words and verses. I began to look for a copy as I visited used bookstores and garage sales. It didn't take long to find one, and I began using it as a reference. One day I noticed an envelope glued to the inside back cover—a found treasure! I eagerly opened this to find a brief, typed letter. The postmark and date on the letter indicated it had been written in 1979. Discovering this letter started an interesting search for more information about the letter's contents.

Evidently, from the letter's wording, the original owner had written to an official of her church inquiring about the reliability of the Amplified Bible. The church leader took the time to answer her questions and stated that while the "mother church" providing oversight had not made an official statement about the version, the founder of their denomination quoted from various versions in writing and speaking. By the fact that the letter had been glued into the back of her copy, I gathered she felt comfortable using it for personal study. I decided to see what I could find out about the church official who responded to the woman's concerns. An Internet search revealed that he wrote an article published in a religious journal and evidently was a trusted and prominent leader.

Not long after that something happened and I remembered this information. We were awaiting the birth of two grandchildren—one in Indiana and the other in Oregon. And we were in California! About two months from the due date, our Oregonian son and his wife received the news that not all was well with their baby. There was a strong possibility that a genetic mutation was present. The doctors warned them that they would face some hard decisions in the near future. As we prayed and waited, our minds went wild with *what if*s and *why*s.

I was traveling for work when we received word that the newest member of our family had arrived early and was being moved by ambulance to a Portland hospital for special neonatal care. Our son drove behind the ambulance alone, leaving his wife in their local hospital to recover from the Cesarean birth. The news from the baby's doctors was not good. They painted a very bleak picture of the baby's future. Should he survive, he would never be alert enough to recognize anyone, he would never speak, or walk.

Chapter 12

Devastated, we prepared to head up to Oregon to give comfort, support, and to share our faith even in tragedy.

As I sought consolation from the Bible, I remembered the Amplified Bible I had recently purchased. Perhaps familiar verses would become even clearer, and I would receive new comfort. Reading Jeremiah 29:11–13 gave me reassuring words:

> For I know the thoughts and plans that I have for you, says the Lord, thoughts and plans for welfare and peace and not for evil, to give you hope in your final outcome. Then you will call upon Me, and you will come and pray to Me, and I will hear and heed you. Then you will seek Me, inquire for, and require Me [as a vital necessity] and find Me when you search for Me with all your heart.

Colin James arrived in a flurry of activity and has remained at the center of a lot of goings-on since his birth. It has not been easy, but God in His infinite mercy and grace has brought so many joys and blessings to our family through this child's special needs that they cannot be counted! Because his condition is so rare, no one can accurately predict what kind of development he will be able to make.

Colin has always been bright-eyed and alert. When he sat up alone, we knew God was continuing to work miracles. Since then we have witnessed miracle after miracle. He developed "Colinnese" (his version of sign language). He took his first steps using a walker, but can now walk alone (unless he wants to speed down school hallways!). Last fall he and Papa sat on the living room sofa, both hard at work playing Angry Birds on their respective tablets.

When Colin scored, he'd lift his fist in the air, make a downward pulling motion and say, "Yes!" As his older brother rolled him onto the floor and playfully lay on top of him, I heard him plead laughingly, "Someone help me here! Please, somebody help!"

In a regular second-grade class now, Colin is active, participating in walkathons using his special walker, snow skiing at Mammoth Mountain, playing at the beach, and traveling to Hawaii for family reunions. He is a joy and a delight to everyone he meets.

The challenging times in your life may not be anything like mine. Your difficulties may come in the form of marital conflict, divorce, death of a spouse, a lost career, life-threatening physical illness, mental disorder, or other trauma. Regardless of the type of difficulty, a woman's self-esteem can suffer while she's living through any of these situations or others. Events in our lives can trigger feeling low self-esteem. It is easy to feel trapped in a seemingly never-ending downward spiral. We may feel that everything is out of our control. When our emotions are raging and our situation seems impossible, our self-confidence may falter. It's often not hard to feel abandoned by everyone, including God. What can we do when life's hard times inevitably happen? There are several questions we can ask ourselves that will help us focus on the right type of things.

First, ask, "How hard is it?" By this I mean that it's OK to acknowledge that what we are facing and going through is hard. Our circumstances are real. You may deal by "not dealing." Pretending that nothing is wrong is unhealthy. However, we cannot stay in this place. Continuing to go over and over things will undermine our self-esteem, leaving us with a lack of trust in our abilities.

The second question we may ask is "How can I move from emotion to action?" It is critical that we decide on a course of action. When we are in the middle of difficult circumstances, regardless of what they are, we can begin to doubt our ability to make good decisions. At that point we begin to believe that there is nothing we can do. That leads to feelings of inadequacy. See how twisted our thinking can become? Taking some kind of action will move us toward a more positive outlook. When our perspective on what is happening is clearer and more defined, our self-esteem will improve. Our actions may seem like only small steps, but those steps can make a difference in our lives. For example, because we were 1,200 miles away, my husband and I felt as if we could do nothing except pray until we realized our oldest granddaughter's birthday was around the corner. We made travel plans and were the birthday girl's party-givers to relieve her parents from all the details. A small action, but one that allowed us to be of help. Our self-esteem will grow as we commit to taking even the small actions. Taking action is important because prolonged periods of emotion can drain even the hardiest of women!

I believe that when we are in the middle of frustrating and traumatic circumstances we need to spend some time reflecting on our past victories. Ask yourself, "How have I overcome situations in the past?" Our answers can bring us strength to face our current challenges. If we can remember other times when things were dark and scary and we survived, then we will be able to be more confident that we can survive the latest problem too. Success leads to more success, and acknowledging past victories will help us believe in our abilities. Positive thinking is not the answer to life's difficult times, but with God's provision, it *can* help!

A woman's self-esteem may fluctuate during hard times, but she needs to realize that God provides what she needs to live her life and survive adversity. We know the priceless value of the Bible, but we often do not use the very words God spoke until our need becomes a desperate one. Then, when we listen to God, we discover His wonders all over again and rediscover the beauty of His written Word. Here are a few passages that I have found helpful as I have faced difficult circumstances.

- HEBREWS 2: 18 (AMP)—"He is able [immediately] to run to the cry of (assist, relieve) those who are . . . [suffering]."
- ISAIAH 41:10 (AMP)—"I will hold you up and retain you with My (victorious) right hand of rightness and justice."
- HEBREWS 13:5 (AMP)—"I will not in any way fail you nor give you up."
- PHILIPPIANS 4:19 (AMP)—"My God will liberally supply (fill to the full) your every need."

So, in preparation for the trials that will come into your life, consider asking, "Will I find God's hand in this experience? Will I be able to learn from it? Will I search God's will for direction and comfort?" Only you can answer these questions. Your self-esteem will become healthier as you grow in your understanding of how God will provide all you need in every situation. Read 1 Peter 3:5 for God's promise to care for us. If you need to refresh your memory of our worth in God's eyes, reread chapter 1!

As God continues to bless our family through Colin's life, we try to be thankful for each and every one of His miracles. We talk about miracles when we see them in someone else's life; experiencing them personally moves us into the realm of praise and amazement at how God works. I am careful to give Him the praise due His name. "And He has put a new song in my mouth, a song of praise to our God" (Psalm 40:3 AMP).

Found Treasure

SUMMING IT ALL UP

I FOUND IT IN THE DRESSER DRAWER I'VE LABELED *Miscellaneous*. It's the drawer that contains odd pieces of jewelry too large to fit in my standing jewelry box on top of the dresser. The drawer holds mementos from the past, like the dried going-away corsage from my wedding. It was in the blue satin, divided box that was originally designed to hold small things such as buttons, nail files, and safety pins. The drawer had become a jumbled box of assorted possessions of no special value or importance. As I was digging for an elusive safety pin, I rediscovered the small, green packet. The packet is only about one-inch square with a snap on the front flap. I found a strange-looking apparatus with two metal parts inside the leather holder. What is it? It's a small, portable safety razor!

It's possible that my razor is a collectible item, and I guess it might have some value. I think an elderly friend in Texas gave it to me years ago. It became a found object that day! A trinket from the past, the leather container has outlived its purpose. With plastic disposable razors available today, it has lost its appeal and usefulness. The convenience factor has been lost in this age of disposability.

Life's interruptions can cause us to step off the path God has shown us. Circumstances such as job loss, marital difficulties, trouble with teenage children, poor health, or bouts of depression can deflect our attention from God's greater purpose for us.

In my search for one object, I found something else, but it had little value. Finding the old razor distracted me from the larger, more important search for the safety pin. I think the same thing happens in my life at times.

There are days when my search for significance is derailed. The end of the day comes, and I realize I have veered off course and have focused on things that have no direct bearing on the tasks I have before me. To help me do what I need to do, I make lists.

I go beyond normal, accepted list-making behavior, however. I may have three or four lists going at one time, not always on paper. I have lists for the week, for each day, for each project. I have actually put "make retreat list" on my general list! At their best, lists are good organizational tools. They can help you stay focused. But when the lists or side trips distract me from the main goal, I can become ineffective rather than purposeful.

Life's interruptions can cause us to step off the path God has shown us. Circumstances such as job loss, marital difficulties, trouble with teenage children, poor health, or bouts of depression can deflect our attention from God's greater purpose for us. As we focus our hearts and minds on God, we will find solutions to our situations. Interruptions are not always negative, and I am not saying that everything in our lives will be resolved. But when we manage to stay focused, we will be able to move forward within God's will. We may not understand the reasons or find complete answers to our questions, but we can continue in the peace only He can give. Our search for identity, meaning, assurance, and contentment will be back on track when we refuse to be diverted.

As I think back to the lessons God has taught me through these found objects, I realize that each lesson has helped me learn how God works in my life—if I allow Him to. By putting myself in the Master Carver's hands, He is free to create something beautiful that will glorify His name. Being on target with what I do and where I go allows God to work through me. Finding all those sand dollars on the beach reminded me that the abilities I have are gifts from God and are meant to be used. Seeing the pewter ring in my jewelry box prompts me to be cautious how I express myself because my words can encourage or condemn.

Lava beds that stretch for miles make a desolate scene but hope flourishes in sighting a lone, green plant surviving against all odds. I am committed to mentoring as a personal mandate and to helping women grow spiritually and develop healthy self-esteem. The child's vintage dress hangs in my guest bedroom serving as a reminder that I should be careful with my relationships. I married a young man whose eternal destination was changed because a small group of believers in Nebraska were faithful to tell others about Jesus. School photos in a shoebox brought back secondhand memories of hard times and a dismal future that were forever changed by God's love and mercy. A beaded bracelet crafted by

You may want to develop a magpie mind. Start your own collection of found treasures and make connections between them and lessons God wants to teach you. Use the space provided at the back of this book to record your finds and the applications God is helping you make. It may be that you cannot take the things you find with you. If that is the case, keep your camera handy and record them. I have done photographic studies in Croatia (balconies), New Orleans (shutters and doors), and England (fences). I am currently collecting "found cemeteries" as I drive back country roads in my new state. Who knows what lessons I will discover or where the journey may lead me?

a 12-year-old boy is a treasured possession because it reminds me that I should never neglect mentoring ministry.

As I think about leaving a strong legacy, I am reminded that it must be an intentional process as I try to live a life that is pleasing to God, one that illustrates what I say I believe. May my signature be as strong and long-lasting as Clemens's was. Finding my grandmother's shorn hair that day was indeed not for the faint of heart! Her determination motivates me to face my own life with courage. The old, damaged quilt lying in pieces taught me that the work women do may fragment their lives and damage their self-esteem. As I use my Amplified Bible with the typed letter in the back, it reminds me to thank God for His tender mercies surrounding my precious grandson.

In her book *The Found Object in Textile Art,* Cas Holmes encourages artists to use found objects in their work to commemorate items that evoke fond memories of travel, relationships, and seen beauty. "Inspiration can be found just about anywhere, even in the most everyday situations. Be inquisitive, ask questions, and set yourself simple challenges to start your observations." She says we need to have "magpie minds!" This is similar to the magpie bird that has a habit of collecting shiny objects. Could it be that God wants us to collect not only things of beauty but by our observations collect lessons He wants to teach us? When you hold your own found objects or look back at the photographs you've taken, and if you are open, God will speak to you. Listening to God speak is the first step to a healthy self-esteem. Lynda Elliott said it very well in *The Counsel of a Friend,* "Only knowing God and experiencing His love can cause us to feel secure. Jesus' shed blood grants us security now and forever. . . . We cannot build our own self-esteem; it must come from God."

From a granite rock to a pewter ring to a quilt piece, found objects can become treasures that enrich our lives and add depth to our souls. And give us stories to tell!

Found Treasure

APPENDIX A

DISCUSSION QUESTIONS

Use the following questions for personal reflection or in a small-group setting.

For a different small-group activity, bring cameras, iPhones, or iPads to photograph found objects women bring for individual self-esteem journals that can be used as guides for personal growth toward more healthy self-esteem.

1. Make a list of objects you have found over time. What spiritual applications can you make about them?

2. What do you think are the top three self-esteem issues women have? How have these impacted your own self-esteem?

3. As a Christian woman, what has God revealed to you about your relationships and how they affect your view of yourself?

4. Which self-esteem issue has caused you the most stress? Why?

5. How do you think your childhood and family life have influenced your self-esteem?

6. Why do you think communication was included as a self-esteem topic?

7. Think about the discussions in this book's 12 chapters. Which require attention for healthy self-esteem in your own life? Is there anything you can do with others to foster self-esteem growth?

A CONVERSATION WITH LINDA

I thought you might be interested in reading some questions I've had about a woman's self-esteem.

1. Why are you interested in the topic of women and self-esteem? Has your self-esteem changed over the years?

Because I enjoy teaching so much, I've had many interesting experiences leading seminars and retreats, as an adjunct seminary professor, and teaching several courses specifically for women. As I've worked with women informally and in more structured environments, I have realized that self-esteem is a huge issue for most women. I've indicated in the chapters of this book that there are many influencers on self-esteem—and I think I've seen all of them at one time or another. God has given us so much through Jesus that it's terrible when a woman is maimed by these issues and can't live her life to the max like God intends. I think that's why I've become more vigilant in my observations and an advocate for women and how they can move toward healthier self-esteem.

In answer to your question about my own self-esteem, I guess it has changed through the years. While I was never what you'd call a supermom, I see now that I did some things right! Even when my children were young, I believe my own childhood molded me for parenting success because my parents were great role models. They encouraged me to pursue a college degree and because of that support, I never questioned my ability to achieve that. The successes I had in college showed me I could pursue postgraduate degrees—although this was years later! As I moved through the demands of those studies, my self-esteem grew, and I began to openly challenge women I met to embrace similar opportunities. All of us have self-esteem issues that vary from time to time and I'm not any different.

2. You spent a lot of time talking about communication. Do you really believe it's that important for a woman's self-esteem?

Actually, I do. Whether it's written, verbal, or nonverbal communication, all of us need to understand how much of our heartache and trouble are caused by failures to communicate. Many years ago, I saw a cartoon drawing of a structure that a committee had built, thinking it knew what the customer wanted. It was ramshackle (that means it wasn't sound and looked terrible) and looked like a committee had built it. The next drawing was what the customer really wanted and showed a tire swinging from a tree rather than an elaborate tree house! I think our communication is like that. We believe we've communicated and end up with irritated neighbors, irate bosses, nonresponsive teenagers, and bewildered spouses. When I realize I haven't communicated, I lose confidence in my relational abilities. If our relationships suffer from communication mishaps, we start believing we are inept. Using the right word at the right time, being careful to say exactly what we mean to say, and clarifying what we hear will help our self-esteem become healthier.

3. Do you think some women's idea of how God sees them is
   wrong?

Well, I certainly think it could be. I've known women who don't
seem to be able to see they are worthy of God's love and consider-
ation. I don't know whether it stems from lack of a strong foundation in God's Word or poor teaching or what. I've been amazed
to hear women talk about how boring their lives are and that they
feel trapped by their life circumstances. They seem unable to
move beyond their past and embrace God's mercy and love. When
I taught a class on self-esteem, I gave my students several fill-in-
the-blank statements and asked them to record their answers.
I prefaced the activity by saying that only God's opinion can provide them with a sure and safe foundation on which to build a
healthy self-esteem. You might like to complete the activity too.

- When I get a compliment, I feel _____

  _____

  _____

  _____

  _____

- When I read or sing about God's love for me, I feel _____

  _____

  _____

  _____

  _____

  _____

- When I am criticized, I feel _____

  _____

  _____

  _____

  _____

- When I do something wrong, I feel _____

  _____

  _____

  _____

- When I think about Jesus' dying for me, I feel _____

  _____

  _____

  _____

- I think when God sees me through His eyes, He . . .
  (choose one.)
  is sorry for me.
  sees a precious creature.
  sees His own image.
  sees a sinful worm.
  is filled with love for me.
  doesn't know who I am.

Your answers to these statements may indicate whether you believe
you are of value to God.

4. You've mentioned several times that our perception of ourselves plays a critical role in our self-esteem. Is there anything practical I can do to change how I think about myself?

What a great question! As I did the research for this book, I found several activities I thought were especially helpful. Here's a compilation of some of them. Set aside a time when you can do this activity without interruption.

• Write down ten good points about yourself. Be honest!

• Write ten negative points about yourself. Be as frank as you can.

- Look at each point and ask yourself, "Is this really true or is it just a belief I picked up which isn't really the way I am?"

- Which list was easier to make? Why do you think this is?

- Go back to your list of negative points. Cross out each word or phrase and write the exact opposite in its place.

- Take each of the new words and use them to finish this sentence: I am _____

    _____

    _____

    _____

    _____

    _____

5. I'm not sure that I agree with you that my self-esteem will influence whether I get involved in ministry. Can you talk about this a little more?

I know that all of us have offered excuses for not becoming involved in ministry. If you're like me, you've probably said, "I'm just too busy right now." I've used my lack of expertise, too, to get out of participating in a project by commenting, "Well, I'd love to do that but I've never done anything in that area before." (And, as my mother would say, "And a little line under that . . . I don't intend to learn how!"). The "reasons" we give for not ministering to others could have an underlying cause—that of low or less-than-healthy self-esteem. The lack of confidence I have in my ability to minister in a situation could really be covering up my fear that I don't measure up. Does that make sense to you? If a woman moves through her home and work life believing she is less than capable, there's not much chance that she'll attempt to reach out to people needing help. So, in the end, it's her self-esteem that keeps her from engaging in activities God may be calling her to do.

Here are some questions you might ask yourself to determine your attitude toward ministry: What ministries am I involved in now? What scares me about moving out of my comfort zone? Does my ministry reflect an acceptance of others or a holier-than-thou attitude? What is my attitude toward those to whom I minister? Have you thought about the example of Christ you portray? List some characteristics Jesus displayed as He ministered to others. Rate how well you demonstrate each one.

6. I work full time outside my home. I would rather be at home, but our family's finances dictate that I work. I am struggling with setting goals that are meaningful. Some weeks my goals revolve around doing all the laundry and paying the bills! Do you have some practical suggestions that might help me?

When my children were still at home, I had several temporary jobs, but I knew there was an end to the craziness on the horizon. However, when my husband was forced to take a medical retirement because of an automobile accident, it became apparent I would have to find a long-term, full-time job. As our family faced some hard financial decisions, my sweet father who had counseled couples as a pastor for many years, helped me develop a plan to help us get through the uncertain weeks and months ahead.

You're right, it's difficult to set goals when you are overwhelmed with daily life and its demands. If you can find a block of time to yourself (maybe a getaway to the library or park or better yet . . . the beach), use the following ideas to get you thinking more long-term. They have helped me. I hope they'll help you too.

• List three new things you'd like to experience this year.

- List three nonfiction books you want to read this year (work-related or of special interest to you).

- List three things about yourself that you want to improve.

- What are your spiritual goals?

- List your family goals for this year. (You have some, right?)

- Name three physical health goals.

- List three work-related goals.

- Name two recreational goals.

- List three financial goals for this year.

After you compose these lists, make some notations about how you can reach the various goals. Remember, if you never start, you'll never reach them. Take small steps. In the end you'll have a healthier self-esteem.

APPENDIX C

GOOD READS

Biehl, Bobb. *Mentoring: Confidence in Finding a Mentor and Becoming One*. Nashville: Broadman & Holman, 1996.

Carter, Donna. *10 Smart Things Women Can Do to Build a Better Life*. Eugene, OR: Harvest House Publishers, 2007.

Chisolm, Gloria. *Forgive One Another: Moving Past the Hurt One Step at a Time*. Colorado Springs: WaterBrook Press, 2000.

Elliott, Lynda D. *The Counsel of a Friend: 12 Ways to Put Your Caring Heart into Action*. Nashville: Thomas Nelson Inc., 1993.

Iorg, Jeff. *Live Like a Missionary*. Birmingham, AL: New Hope Publishers, 2011.

Kelley, Rhonda H. *True Contentment: A Biblical Study for Achieving Satisfaction in Life*. Birmingham, AL: New Hope Publishers, 2010.

Kok, Elsa. *A Woman with a Past, A God with a Future*. Birmingham, AL: New Hope Publishers, 2006.

Kroeger, Catherine, and James R. Beck. *Healing the Hurting: Giving Hope to Abused Women*. Grand Rapids, MI: Baker Books, 1998.

Leadingham, Everett. *Me I See: A Christian Approach to Self-Esteem.* Kansas City, MO: Beacon Hill Press, 1994.

Lee, Wanda. *The Story Lives On: God's Power Throughout Generations.* Birmingham, AL: New Hope Publishers, 2012.

Leman, Kevin. *Smart Women Know When to Say No.* Grand Rapids, MI: Revell, 2010.

Lieberman, David. *Instant Analysis.* New York: St. Martin's Press, 1998.

Mindell, Phyllis. *How to Say It for Women: Communicating with Confidence and Power Using the Language of Success.* New York: Prentice Hall Press, 2001.

Nutt, Grady. *Being Me.* Nashville: Broadman Press, 1971.

Sweet, Leonard. *The Jesus Prescription for a Healthy Life.* Nashville: Abingdon Press, 1996.

Thomas, Donna S. *Faces in the Crowd: Reaching Your International Neighbor for Christ.* Birmingham, AL: New Hope Publishers, 2008

Woman's Missionary Union. *Tell the Story: A Primer on Chronological Bible Storying.* Birmingham, AL: Woman's Missionary Union, 2012. Go to wmu.com or call 1-800-968-7301 to order.

Words to Live by for Women. Brentwood, TN: Bethany House, 2004.

Resources to Strengthen and Equip You!

Real Women
Leading With Proverbs 31 Values
LISA TROYER AND DAWN YODER
ISBN: 978-1-59669-396-8
N144105 • $14.99

Journey to Confidence
Becoming Women of Influential Faith
KIMBERLY SOWELL
ISBN: 978-1-59669-389-0
N134130 • $14.99

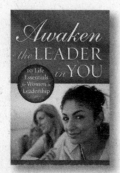

Awaken the Leader in You
10 Essentials for Women in Leadership
DR. LINDA M. CLARK
ISBN: 978-1-59669-221-3
N084144 • $12.99

Unlocked
5 Myths Holding Your Influence Captive
CYNTHIA CAVANAUGH
ISBN: 978-1-59669-385-2
N134126 • $14.99

Available in bookstores everywhere. For information about these books or our authors, visit NewHopeDigital.com. Experience sample chapters, podcasts, author interviews and more! Download the New Hope app for your iPad, iPhone, or Android!